GET OUT OF YOUR COMFORT ZONE

The exercises and descriptions are based on the experiences of the authors and were selected with great care. However, only you can decide, if the exercises fit into your life situation and if you want to do them. We don't assume any liability for any drawbacks or damages, that result from the exercises in this book.

ISBN-13: 978-1466262874

ISBN-10: 1466262877

Sascha Ballach / Andreas Brede

GET OUT OF YOUR COMFORT ZONE

The Exercise Book for your Personal Growth

Table of Contents

Praise for the German Book

"I had a lot of fun while working through the exercises of this book and I am very delightet. My life has improved through it very much. I am able to handle new situations much easier and I like to experience unfamiliar and exciting situations, which I wouldn't have done at all before. I enjoy my life much more now and every day turned into an exciting adventure for me. Even though there was a certain inhibition level at first, this book is called „get out of your Comfort Zone" for a reason. Some exercises did make me chuckle, since I felt uncomfortable with them. But after all it were exactly those exercises that I had the most fun with. I can recommend this book to everyone, who wants to get more involved with the topic of personal development. The author explains, how change takes place and how we can achieve it, in a very easy and understandable way. He leaves out unnecessary excesses and comes right to the point. This book has helped me to feel more happy almost every day and has even made me a little addicted to making new experiences. Whoever wants and expects more from life, should read this book. For me this is definitely the most effective book on this topic I have read up to now."

"Beforehand I want to say, this book is definitely not for people who are too concerned about what other people, even total stranges, might think of them. True to the motto „embarrass yourself daily", the authors provide a large collection of more or less unusual exercises for expanding your horizon. One thing is guaranteed: Whoever let's himself get involved in this game, will make new experiences, reduce inhibitions and discover new possibilities of how life can also be. Honestly, to me, too, a lot of the exercises seem so unusual, absurd and outside the normal acting, that it's quit hard for me to even start doing them. But eventually - and I have to admit that to the authors - it has a lot to do with my Comfort Zone. This book is refreshingly different, radical, and for sure not for wimps. And not despite of this, but exactly because of this, I give 5 full stars and the good advice (also to myself): Don't just read, do it!"

"I think this book is good and helpful for readers with appropriate expectations. It's certainly not a scientific reference book and it's probably not supposed to be. What I find even almost more exciting than the book itself, are the scattered critical reviews on this site. For me, the examples that are mentioned there, as well as the fact, that one of these reviews gets over 100 positiv votes from amazon visitors that probably don't even know the book, is a wonderful illustration of the Comfort Zone itself. It also

shows how relieved some people are, when they find a reason to not have to leave their own Comfort Zone."

"These two NLP trainers come to the point! I have to do it, with a lot of examples, e.g. I approached „Heinz Becker" in a Hotel because of this book. I am so exited that I will present this book to my association! For me the book is a good manual how to live. How Johann Wolfgang von Goethe said: „It is not enough to know, you also have to apply it; it is not enough to want, you also have to do it." With big interest I read about the limbic system and I understood it without having to complete studies in neurology. The book is in my TOP 10 list, very recommendable in my world!"

"If you deal with the topic of personal development and browse through the common literature, you often find the same subjects and a lot of books are simply repetitions of concepts you've already read for a thousand times. Here it is different! Andreas and Sascha have managed to create a completely new concept and also to make it easy to understand for everyone. What was akways missing, was a guideline, that takes me further step by step. So it mostly stayed at a solo run. This missing link (the step by step guideline) is filled by this book. I'm sill at the beginning of the book, but the exercises, that I have done so far, have totally convinced me. It's just fun to go through life beeing happier, and that's exactly what one achives through this book. Tackle and master challenges and achieve results. Sometimes it's easier and sometimes it's harder, but in the end you are proud of yourself to have put you to the challenge. I can absolutely recommend this book and hope, that it might help everybody even just a little bit to live a better life."

"Get out of your Comfort Zone" is finally a book, that one doesn't want to put away after the first few pages, since the tips and instructions are doable and the background is described in a good way. This book was created through the own experiences of the authors, unlike alot of other books about personal development. As a reader it doesn't only want me to read through the whole book, but also to really start to change things in my life, to grow and to try out new things. Because what is more exciting than to get out of one's usual territory and to expand the own Comfort Zone? If you aren't only interested in personal development on the edge, but want to experience and implement it actively, this is a good guidance to start with the adventure of „getting out of your comfort zone". In this book everyone can find exercises according to their own most important area, where they want to start changing themselves. I can really recommend this: dare it and start!"

www.comfortzonebook.com

"A fascinating book with a lot of refreshing suggestions and tips. Designed humorously. Promising in every way! However, most of the exercises require a lot of time. Still very recommendable!"

"The NLP trainers Andreas Brede and Sascha Ballach show you in this book, how easy it is to make everyday life more interesting. In the process, the one or other positive change will silently sneak into your life. That's the one impact this book can have on you. The other Possibility: You know exactly, what you want to optimize on yourself. For example to achieve more success when flirting. In this case, you search for the suiting exercise in the book and just do it. Exercises... one or the other might think now, exercises... And exactly at this point the competence of Sascha Ballach and Andreas Brede applies. What these two label as exercises is probably not what you imagine it to be. Because to exercise with the content of the book you don't need anything. Neither incense sticks, nor a soundproof room or the right pitch for the ever-lasting Om. The only thing that can help you, is to walk through your day with open eyes, just taking in everything that you perceive and   transforming it in a new setting into a mighty tool for yourself. An example? Maby for the first flirting step? Smile at strangers, Just smile!"

"For the next four weeks smile at all the people that you meet. Thereby your smile should come from deep inside you. Watch people's reaction to it while doing so. Smile also in difficult situations, that can occur at your job or in everyday life. This is really simple. And that is why we recommend this book as a gift. Because what is better than seeing the shining eyes of the presentee, when success has come into reach."

"I think this book is great. Everything is described in a good way and the exercises make sense, even though it might be hard for the one or the other in the beginning, but exactly that's the point. I can recommend this book to everyone who wants to expand their comfort zone."

"A few weeks ago I had the new book of Sascha Ballach in my mailbox and then didn't give it out of my hands again - that means: I read this book in one evening! But caution! „Get out of your Comfort Zone" has severe side effects. If you DON'T want to change you should better not take this book to hand or even worse - work with it... Because since then this book lies on my desk and I work with it actively every day! I have done that with little books up to now. If I look at my big book shelf with all the books about personal development, what struck me while reading „Out of your Comfort Zone" is: this book is pleasantly different. The ingredients of this book have a

lot of positive side effects that show after some time of taking it regularly! This book is NOT the famous „painkiller" or a „cure-all", instead it deals with the things at its root and gives longterm solutions rather than short-term clever tips... But now something about the contents."

"I first got in touch with the topic of „Getting out of your Comfort Zone" two years ago in a seminar with Sascha Ballach and through his forum that goes by the same name. Instead of theories and any kind of clever wisdoms, the focus was always only on one thing: to start taking action. To achieve this there were and are a lot of practical exercises, that challenged me in the last two years, that contributed to my personal development and that made my heart beat more than once. But when I look back, all the exercises had one thing in common... they extremely expanded my comfort zone and made me feel more free in my life! In my opinion the book is a logical consequence of continuing this exciting topic."

"Get out of your Comfort Zone" is divided into two parts. One short theoretical part about the human personality and about personal development and a second long practical part! Yes exactly: this book is absolutely a work book... a workshop that gives the reader enough exercises and tasks for weeks. These exercises all have one goal or one effect: all exercises produce more flexibility in your own personality, more selection options in your actions and more flexibility. After I read the theoretical part pretty fast, I went on to part 2, the part with the many exercises and variations that Sascha suggests to do to expand your Comfort Zone. Here I notice the primarily practical approach of Sascha Ballach: He has done the exercises himself, so he speaks from his own experiences and from the experiences of the participant in his Comfort Zone forum. In the last couple weeks I have done a variety of exercises. I have integrated them into my life and my conclusion is: Absolutely awesome book! Good impact and a lot of fun reading and doing it!"

"Right after reading the introduction to the exercises, the underlying message was totally clear to me and I felt the drive to start right away. Now I don't even have to think about how I will get out of my comfort zone anymore, instead I get so many pages with exercises that I will work through step by step. Wonderful book that helps me to reduce personal fears. Now I have no more excuses. Thank you"

"After an introduction to the topic of personal development and comfort zone, there are exercises and tips to leave your comfort zone. These are very multifaceted, so there was also something for me to begin with. A few exercises, with which hesitated

I at first, made my comfort zone grow a whole lot. I'm already looking forward to the next exercises, and I leave my comfort zone again and again!"

"Hereby I create my first review on amazon and to do this it needed a very special book. Personaly I have already read hundreds of books about personal development and have visited about fifty seminars and I can say that this book is something special. It focuses on two main points: the fear, that stops us from becoming the person that we want to be and the best (maby even the only) possibility for us to develop is to take action! In the first part of the book the two authors manage to explain the most important basics in a short and entertaining way and to motivate the reader to start to take action.
In the second part of the book is a presentation of a lot of exercises, that will guide you on your own path of personal development step by step. I have personaly already done alot of the exercises that are descibed in the book and I could see positive results of learning success and change. I recommend this book to anybody who wants to develop, especially through the only real way promising: by doing and taking action! How fast it can happen, that we always go the same paths. From musical genre to culinary taste! The authors of this book make diverse suggestions to discover NEW things and to get out of the Comfort Zone while doing so. What I like? The ideas are doable and encourage to find own ideas. The idea book is totally recommendable."

"The book is easy and refreshing to read. The big type helps to read fast through the book. It is explained that the cause of our inflexibility (fear of the unknown) is the limbic system. It is necessary to change the structure of it. For this there is the practical part of the book. The exercises are indeed doable, partially amazingly easy and still effective and they have a high potential of fun. If an exercise does cause too much fear, I recommend the hypnosis CD of Chris Mulzer: RESOLVE YOUR FEAR. I have already made several exercises, but I am still in the course of doing it. This book will probably last a year, then I will need replenishment. :-)"

"Get out of your Comfort Zone" since I know what this means, for me, really a lot has happened and I was, and still am, totally surprised about how fast and easy change can happen! The book is a good opportunity to expand my Comfort Zone even further and with it to design my life even better, and especially: to have fun changing. While reading the book I had a few aha moments, and I realized for myself where I have already expanded my Comfort Zone, but even more, how much potential there still is! The numerous exercises are easy and understandably described and really

make you want to try them out right away. Some are real challenges... but that's why the book is called „Get out of your Comfort Zone"!

"If you want to make your life better and more intense and especially, if you want to change while having a lot of fun, then this book is the right reading for you. Buy it, read it, try it... embellish life. Actually pretty easy :)"

"I am excited about this book - in 2007 I came to the subject area of social fear and comfort zone expansion through the PickupCommunity - here I did programs like „Demonic Confidence" and in this book I find a lot of these things, too. It contains 100 apparent exercises that bring everyone to their borders. I'm only missing the really hard exercises (dancing in the pedestrian area etc...) but the ones described in the book are therefor more practical. I can unconditionaly recommend this book. One more thing: It's not a book for reading - it's a book for doing. After 15 minutes you are through the introduction and explanation of about 20 pages - after that it's only about doing - there is nothing more to read. THAT'S how books have to be ;P"

"Children show us the way: Full of curiosity and thirst for action they explore the world, want to know and experience everything. Often we have to stop them and pull them back into „our world". Children have the best ideas and dare to go into parts of the world fearlessly, that we as adults often only want to look at from a distance. Here also we often hold them back and program them to how dangerous the world can be. Over time - and to not feel excluded from society through not beeing obedient - we, as children, forget how fearless we once explored our world as we go along, how every day was full of adventure and how easy certain things were, with which we struggle so much as adults.
The authors of the exercise book "Get out of your Comfort Zone" give us a tool, with which we can experiment in life again. In about 100 exercises in all kinds of categories of life (e.g. social contacts, daily routines, self confidence, relationships...) everybody can accomplish many tips and especially tasks, that not only enrich your life, but also let's you see it from a different perspective, the way we have already done it daily when we were children: to see life as a big playground with endless possibilities. Thank you for this work!"

www.comfortzonebook.com

Introduction

At the age of 12 I started getting very involved with personal development. Since then, I've spent more than 50,000 Euros for seminars, books, cassette and video courses. In spite of this, I have experienced little success. In the mean time, I've met many people, who shared this experience. They, after attending many seminars, and reading certain books, did so without feeling any progress. But I could not and did not want to be content with this.

Through my work as an assistant of a well-known NLP and personality trainer, and long-time leader and organizer of a NLP peer group, I had the opportunity to observe many people with their development. Whose development was pronounced, and how long did it take? Why did one person's development occur more quickly and more intensely? Why do some people seem to see great changes, while others do not? And in which situations have I sensed a great deal of development myself?

After years of observation and study, the simple solution became clear. We always develop ourselves if we step outside our comfort zone. That sounds so simple, and it is- if only it weren't for that little word if.

What is your comfort zone? Simply put, your comfort zone is everything that you have experienced, and where you feel comfortable. Unfortunately, it is not always so easy to escape. If you are like most people, you probably find reasons for not doing certain things. Reasons like, "Oh, that sounds too simple, that can't really work," "Why is that supposed to help? That has nothing to do with my problem," etc...

But our excuses are not the only things that keep us from getting out of our comfort zones. Often we simply don't see the opportunities. We always need people around us who help show us these opportunities.

I have put together over 100 exercises and additional variations, which over the course of time should help you to step outside of your comfort zone. I am sure that there are also some exercises that won't help you bring you out of your comfort zone. This couldn't be avoided, because

this book is made for everyone. Nevertheless, please do all of the exercises. This way, you will avoid skipping an exercise that is very good for you. Do the exercises as they are described, and then try out the variations. Maybe you can come up with some of your own variations as well.

With this kind of exercise, the experience of going through the exercise first-hand is crucial. You can't always logically estimate what an exercise will do for you. That's what makes life interesting- you never know what comes next.

To get the most out of them, after doing an exercise, answer the following questions for yourself (preferably in writing):

• How was I doing before the exercise? What was I thinking and feeling?

• How was I doing during the exercise? What was I thinking and feeling?

• How am I doing after the exercise? What am I thinking and feeling?

• If I had to do the exercise again, how would I think and feel then?

I have done almost all of the exercises myself. Most of them were also done by friends, acquaintances, or participants in the comfort zone forum. In doing so, I've gained a really deep knowledge and experience in this area, so that the exercises are really hands-on. During my research, I constantly stumbled upon exercises relating to the comfort zone, which upon a closer look, are clearly rooted in theory, not in practice. But that is not the case in this book. You can trust that all of the exercises are practice-oriented, and doable.

Depending on your own state of development, some of the exercises might be fairly easy for some, and for others incomparably difficult. This is good, because it gives us a taste of the whole spectrum of human development. I cannot imagine a world where conformity is the order of the day. Lastly, these exercises should really help you to lead an exciting life, where suddenly many things are possible, and even more things become easy.

During the exercises you will be confronted with yourself, with your personality, with your feelings, and with your fears. An emotional roller coaster ride is nothing out of the ordinary when doing the exercises. But the number of positive things that come out of these exercises cannot be overestimated.

I am sure of one thing: it is unbelievably fun to do the exercises, to be able to watch yourself as your own personality develops, and to successfully embark upon a journey of your own...

PS: Perhaps you have noticed that we, Andreas and Sascha, have written the whole book using the first-person singular, even though we are two authors. We did this for several reasons. First, we found it difficult to always distinguish who was speaking, since we wrote the whole book together, and have so many shared experiences. Earlier on, we had always switched back and forth between I (Sascha), and I (Andreas), which in our opinion resulted in more confusion than clarity. We also find it more personal writing this way. We will address you personally, and we will also be as personal as we can be.

The Fear of the Unknown

In so many of the "how-to-manuals", we read that change is easy. Yet for most of us, it is both difficult to change intentionally, and to handle change from outside. How come? Are we weak? No, we just need a lesson on the structure of our brains.

The brain has developed over the course of billions of years. In the process, it has not been invented again and again from scratch, but instead it has accumulated new parts over the course of time, the most recent of which is the neocortex, which is found in mammals, and is especially large in humans. But long before this, around 3.5 billion years ago, the limbic system came into being. This has a much greater influence upon our behavior than most of us are aware of.

Because of our superior intelligence we often think that we should be able to just decide something, and just like that it ought to be set in motion. But when we consider the New Year's resolutions that we might have made, we see that it doesn't work like that. Maybe it was the resolution to quit smoking, to do more sports, or to lose weight. But, if we are honest, how often has this worked? Why is it so hard for us to make changes with will power alone? We are fully aware that these changes would be good for us, and still we are unable to see them through. If only our intellect were responsible for our behavior, then we would be able to accomplish any task that we undertook.

It is our limbic system which makes this impossible. It determines our behavior much more decisively than we think. It does this to give us security- the security of survival. So it adapts working strategies, and applies them over and over again. The consequence of this is that it makes us continue to act pretty much in the same way as we always have, since we have always managed to get by in this way. The limbic system isn't interested in us reaching our optimal performance. Every change means danger, and the limbic system can't decide whether this change will protect us or endanger us. So by default, it attempts to keep things going the same way as they always have. In our fast paced day, this time honored strategy persists- but little by little to our disadvantage. The world

around us is changing quickly. We are constantly confronted with new situations. Many of our grandparents worked their entire lives in one job in one company. Today this would be unthinkable. Changing our employer, and even our occupation, is common for us all. But the limbic system struggles with changes like these; so many times it decides to continue doing something that we don't really want to do. It also makes sure that our consciousness supports these decisions.

So we find good reasons for us not to change our job, although we would like to change it. We also find good excuses for continuing to smoke, maybe because we're afraid that if we quit, we'll no longer have access to the information which we receive from our colleagues, only during smoke breaks. It can also occur with the comfort zone exercises, that you find an excuse for not doing a certain exercise. Most likely your limbic system made this decision, and your consciousness supports it, finding good reasons for doing so.

So I recommend that you do every exercise, regardless of what line of reasoning your consciousness gives you. Observe what you think and feel, and bit by bit you should be able to see a pattern. Very often we always behave in the same way, when this fear of the unknown comes to the surface. And we might always have a similar rationale, similar thoughts, and so on, whenever confronted with the unknown.

The great thing is that in other situations, we can easily recognize, when our limbic system has made a decision, which our consciousness then tries to justify. Once we are aware of this, we have the opportunity to really think the situation through, and to determine whether we want to do something or not, independent of our fears. Often the fear is irrational, and merely blocks our path. Through these comfort zone exercises, we will learn how to recognize these fears, and to decide on purpose, whether to give in to them, or to change something for a better tomorrow.

You should also be aware of another thing. The limbic system has another function- it filters information. Every second, we are confronted with more than 1,000 pieces of information. Our brain is not able to process all of these, so the information is filtered, and only the most im-

portant pieces of information are allowed to get through to us. But who decides which information is important? Have you ever decided which information is important for you, and which isn't? The limbic system makes this decision for you.

A few years ago, I was unhappy with my job, and an acquaintance offered me a very interesting job. He spoke with me about it in Thailand. I forgot about the conversation afterwards. Then he sent me an e-mail, where he asked me and some others, what we thought of the offer. I answered this e-mail thoroughly, at least I thought I did, but I completely overlooked the question about the job. Some time later, I was on the phone with the man, and he spoke to me directly about the job again. I was dumbfounded. I couldn't believe that he had asked me that in his e-mail. Naturally I checked it out, and he was right. It was really in the e-mail. And I also looked at my answer. I had answered all questions that came before and after, but I didn't notice this one question. Fortunately, he was persistent-otherwise I would have ended up giving this dream job to someone else.

The same thing can happen to you, say, when you are looking through your favorite newspaper, and you overlook an easily visible ad, where the job of your dreams is described. Somehow it just gets filtered out. So sometimes it is worth it to have your partner look through the paper, to look for something that is interesting for you. He or she has different filters from yours, and is able to notice different things.

As your limbic system gradually learns that new things are good for you, and that they, too, help you to survive, and when you are open for new and unfamiliar things, then the filter mechanisms will change. You will suddenly notice all kinds of exciting and new things in the world, with all of the opportunities that come with them. The comfort zone exercises that come later on in this book are the perfect training program for this.

Once you begin to regularly confront yoursef with your fears, you will soon notice that they also have an influence on other areas of your life. All of my life I had the fear of heights. I wouldn't let this keep me from climbing trees or going up the T.V. tower, but I still had weak knees when doing so. While my friends were climbing the trees in seconds, going from branch to branch, I would be slowly and carefully taking every

step, testing every branch again and again. Once in a more stable position, I would be content to linger there for a while, before beginning my descent. For a long time, I didn't give this fear much thought, because it didn't come up so often. But I have been working on other fears. So recently, I was in the Elbe Sandstone Mountains with some friends, climbing up the iron way (in Italian, via ferrata). It was certainly quite an experience for me, which I think is only natural, when you are climbing about ten meters high without any security, on slippery steps made of iron. Despite this, I didn't sense any of my fear of heights. No more weak knees. I had respect of the height, so I didn't become overconfident, but I could tell that the fear was gone. Who knows what other fears have also parted along the way?

To make this experience possible for you, we have made the comfort zone exercises as comprehensive as possible. We have incorporated things pertaining to many areas of life. So hopefully, while you work on conquering different fears, you will be able to deal with others as well.

The Model of the Comfort Zone

In Germany we often use the term, Alltag, literally all-day, which means, everyday life, or daily routine. But what does this term really mean for us? Does it mean that "all" days are the same? I think that the term itself is very misleading, and even dangerous. It seems like it means that every day can be the same. Also, it conveys a false sense of security- a security that no longer exists in today's world.

As already mentioned in other parts of the book, the world is whirling with change. Even if we do adhere to our routines and habits, we'll never be able to change the world with them. The possibility for change rests with us- with our decisions, and which path we choose to take.

Here are a few examples of the changes taking place in the world around us:

The Workplace

Industrial society has gone from being a service society to being an information society. Some industries completely vanished. Factories and job opportunities are being moved from one country to another. Jobs that have always been considered secure, like working at the bank, have become unpredictable. There is no such thing as a secure position any more. The world of work is changing at a breathtaking speed.

Demography

The population is becoming older, causing the proportion of men to women to become increasingly unequal. The population in Asia is growing faster than that in European countries. In Germany there will be less people in the future than there are now.

Technology

There are more and more sophisticated technical solutions. In the mean time, we are chatting, e-mailing, telephoning, skyping, or sending one another SMS's, sometimes even simultaneously. Nanotechnology has become an old hat- now genetic engineering presents completely new challenges, related to ethical and moral questions.

Those are just some changes that perhaps on the surface have nothing to do with you or your situation. But they really do present us with changes that affect all of our lives. No longer can someone have complete control in all areas of his life. Life has become too complex. Now the question arises, how we will deal with all of this knowledge, and with all of the changes in the world.

www.comfortzonebook.com

The Comfort Zone

The comfort zone is the "feel good zone"- the place where you feel secure and comfortable. In your comfort zone, your habits and routines at home and in your life are organized in a certain way. Sounds pretty good, huh?

The comfort zone gives us security. Generally, you can predict fairly well how it will turn out if you do something a certain way, and you adjust accordingly. We avoid, as much as possible, actions with negative effects. The comfort zone is what we are familiar with. Our habits and routine, in turn, are controlled by the unconscious mind, which has been constantly exposed to many influences since our birth (and probably also before). From a certain age you became aware of your identity. The identity formation happens along with being able to distinguish between "we" and "I." You learn that you can act of your own accord. And you learn that your actions have consequences. You organize your life by referring to these consequences, which are determined by your environment,

The deceptive thing is that at this early age your environment, in the form of your parents, friends, and schoolmates, or other people, gives you the feedback. Naturally, and as is proper, your boundaries are established for you when you are a child. This is definitely positive. Not crossing the street on red helps you to survive, in any case. On the other hand, these boundaries also determine the constraints in your life. As you must already know, everyone has different boundary lines, because everyone's surroundings are different, and everyone has different experiences. But these experiences are ultimately the foundation for your habits and routines.

Generally, everyone avoids every action, which in a given situation in life has negative consequences or makes them feel bad. While still young, one is not yet aware that the same action in other surroundings could possibly have positive consequences. With every experience you go through, your picture of the world is being built or changed.

The comfort zone is your model of the world.

"Every experience changes your perception of the world."

Perhaps as you read the line, you already could envision the implications. If every experience changes your world, then it must be possible for you to change your life in a certain direction through hand-picked experiences. And this is right. The more that you experience, the more the way you look at the world changes.

Unfortunately no sure formula exists. It is not possible to say, that if I do A, then B will follow. Because of the variety of every individual's experiences, and the level of their development, every experience is interpreted differently, in their world.

What is outside of the comfort zone?

Often, the comfort zone is described as a model comprised of three areas: the comfort zone, the risk zone, and the panic zone. In this model, the risk zone begins outside of the comfort zone, where the changes take place. When passing a certain threshold in the risk zone, you enter the panic zone.

However, this model implies that every change is associated with risk. Of course this is not the case, even if some would be borders of your known world. For some changes you will certainly need to be willing to trade your security for something unfamiliar, without knowing if this will help you in any way or not. But more often then not you will have fun while making changes. I have asked a lot of people for what reasons they like to change themselves, and for many of them having fun while doing so is their greatest motive.

You can't know beforehand, what kind of impact an experience outside your comfort zone will have on you. You can surely think a lot about what might happen to you, but only through experiencing it yourself you will get the insight. Here I'm not talking about making all kinds of experiences just for the sake of the experience. As I have already mentioned in other parts of the book, you are responsible yourself in which direction you want to change your life. It should be clear to you, that it shouldn't be any experiences that could harm e.g. your health. Not every experi-

www.comfortzonebook.com

ence has to be made. But it's worth it to question yourself and for what reason you don't want to make a certain experience. Is it fear that stops you from doing it, or is it your free decision? Because here you define the borders of you comfort zone... and with it your world.

How do I realize the borders of my comfort zone?

The realization of borders is actually pretty easy. The borders of your comfort zone are the borders of what is familiar to you. I can give you something help for the exercise part of the book. There are two ways you can tell that something is holding you back:

* You sense an uncomfortable feeling. This is a clear signal that some-where you are outside the borders of your comfort zone. As soon as you notice this feeling, decide quickly how you can use this signal as an indicator to get out of your comfort zone, through an "unfa-miliar" action.

* You supposedly know why exactly you don't have to do a certain exercise, and that it won't do anything for you. Again: only through self-made experiences can you expand your comfort zone, and with it, your world.

Perhaps it would be simpler to describe the theme with a comparison. The boundaries of your comfort zone correspond with the limitations under which you live. Are there areas where you can't operate as freely as you'd like? And what is hindering you from doing something? These are the boundaries of your comfort zone. So every expansion of these boundaries is a step in the direction of a self-determined life. Life is self-determined, for example, when the decisions and actions are not based upon fear.

Applications

Exercises for expanding the comfort zone are found almost everywhere.
They can even be found in more conservative areas like business ma-
nagement, or in modern psychotherapy. That is not surprising, since in
these areas, effect is in the foreground.

Shyness

According to a study conducted by Bernardo Carducci, the leader of the
Shyness Research Institute at Indiana University, 45-50% of the population suffers from shyness. Of these, between around 15-20% are extremely effected, and suffer from severe effects such as stuttering or blushing,
cannot keep eye contact, or seldom laugh. The others who are affected
are known as secretly shy people.

At the same time, shyness is seldom taken seriously, even though it can
lead to social isolation. It is one of the destructive emotions, and ham-
pers one's development, and can limit one's possibilities in life. Naturally,
all of us can be shy in certain situations. I have designed the practice
section of the book so that there are exercises in every section relating
to this theme.

Psychotherapy

In psychotherapy, especially in behavioral therapy, it has long been well
known in certain areas of therapy, that changes on the relational level
have massive impact on the internal state. Behavior therapy originated
from the findings of scientific psychology. These forms of treatment are
not problem centered, but proceed from a background of study. That
means that cause study is not necessarily performed, but more constructively rather, the focus is on working on the fears themselves.

One typical thematic area which is treated with comfort zone exercises
is social phobias. Here one is confronted with the fear-causing stimulus,
for example, by standing on a raised platform in the middle of the super

market, and singing songs or reciting poetry. In the case of strong phobias, the treating therapist is often present to give support if it is needed. Later, the exercise is done alone. Once successful conquering one fear, other aspects of the fear can be addressed as well.

Flirting

I first became aware how great the demand is for advice in the area of flirting, while conducting my research for this book. A whole scene has developed around flirting, called Pick Up Artists. Many TV channels, like MTV, have also taken up this theme.

In the flirt scene, many methods and techniques are learned, to help someone achieve success with the opposite sex, by acting in a certain way. It is my opinion, that in this and in other areas of life as well, it is not enough merely to learn certain techniques by memory, even if they apparently work at first. At some point, you can no longer hide your personality behind technique. And at this point, if not sooner, the other party loses interest.

So clearly the development of one's own personality is the better choice. And this development never ends- you always have areas where you aren't yet meeting your potential.

The professional flirting industry is separated into various groups. One is composed of people, who as far as I can tell, want to have success with gimmickry and cheap tricks, who subordinate their behaviors and their personality to correspond to the goal at hand, in order to achieve successful results, which are as measurable as possible. Naturally, such extreme behavior changes the feedback of the opposite sex, possibly in a positive direction. But then we come to the fundamental consideration, namely whether only being interested in achieving a certain goal isn't very superficial in this case. Everyone has to decide this for themselves.

The second group, as I see it, is composed of people, who have recognized that merely learning techniques and methods doesn't bring lasting results. Surprisingly, many of these how-to-books are riddled with a smorgasbord of different techniques for change; many of them taken out

of other areas, but nevertheless, in effect, are based upon another approach.

How would it be to see one's own change not only confined to this aspect, but as a complete, holistically "complete package," with the aim of further developing one's personality? After all, our life is composed of many moments and events…

Business management

"Get the workers out of the comfort zone" was the title of a report in Manager Magazin, a German periodical. According to this report, a high feeling of security hinders productivity, so company leadership should also expose their workers to situations with an element of fear. Whoever has a secure position should count himself fortunate, because as I mentioned earlier, change has made its entrance into the working world.

In this book, I follow a fundamentally different approach, which is based upon voluntary change that comes from within. The comfort zone exercises are so effective, that they will show enormous effect directly in one's professional life, in areas such as making contacts, fighting avoidance strategies, etc. A relaxed worker, who is not inhibited by fear, is without doubt a great asset to the productivity of any company.

Whoever ventures out into self-employment will have to be able to get out of his comfort zone time and time again. The entrepreneur is always confronted with his own boundaries. Through practice, automatic strategies can be established, which will constructively support you in your work.

www.comfortzonebook.com

Imprinting and Conditioning

"Who am I?" is probably the most common question ever asked.

I know certain people who are against changing, and who try with all of their might never to change, because they want to be "true to themselves." But of course, even these people change, since their environment changes. The changes happen simply from outside, and they have to react to them. But what does it mean to be true to oneself?

To answer this question, I have to look back and describe some of the facets of early personality development. After being born, we are strongly dependent upon our parents and their care. Memories about life before the age of four are almost impossible to recollect, since our brain saves this information in a different way from later on, and we forget how to recall these memories.

From a certain point on our identity is formed, and we recognize that we are our own individual person, an "I," and not a "We". Science offers us several models, as to when a child forms his own identity. Some psychologists claim that the formation of the identity is connected with our first lies, through which we recognize that our parents do not think like we do, do not know everything, and that we have something which distinguishes us from our environment.

In our childhood, our values and character qualities are formed through our upbringing, which from a certain age is determined not only by our parents, but also by kindergarten or school. This is a conditioning process similar to the training of dogs. Through the connection of cause and effect, we learn that what happens as a consequence of not doing our homework, forgetting to clean our rooms, making our clothes dirty, etc. Certain invisible rules are established, which are not consciously accessible to us. These are the experiences which shape us.

So what does it mean, under these circumstances, to be "true to oneself"? As I described in the last section, it is even truer that much of what we believe is our world has been predefined for us from outside.

The conditioning of our childhood is still in effect, as well as the imprinting from our social surroundings. Seen this way, we are actually not ourselves, but products of the conditioning and imprinting process which we have undergone. Later on, we have our own experiences of course, for example, in relationships, or at work, but our conditioning and imprinting are still resonating, help to form our basic presuppositions.

Because everyone's has a different environment, and some people come from completely different cultures, everyone is obviously exposed to different conditioning and imprinting. Therefore the world is seen differently through the eyes of everyone. I am amazed sometimes, that many people voluntarily accept the perspective of others, adopting them in their own world.

Then how do we manage to lead a self determined life, acting independently, with our own way of thinking? It is actually rather simple: we must undo the conditioning received from our environment, which independently determines our choices. We no longer want to be dependent upon predetermined rules from outside, which usually turn up as unseen limitations in our lives.

The only thing that helps is when we take our development into our own hands, and start to form our world on the level of self determined experiences. Although perhaps some of the exercises in the next part will seem at first glance to be of trivial importance, when taken as a whole, the practice part of the book is a complete training program, with which you can develop your personality. Expect everything in your life to change, as soon as you determine the direction you are going.

www.comfortzonebook.com

Habits

How often do you think about how you walk? I pretty much never do, since I learned it at some point, and now it comes automatic. We all have similar automatically executed abilities, which we all learned at some point, and which we no longer have to think about. What happens, though, when we have to change something?

Years ago I had a mountain bike with cage pedals. Those are the pedals, into which you can slip your shoe, so that your shoe can't slip so easily off of the pedal. This is a great advantage when cycling in the countryside. To come out of these pedals, I always had to pull my foot backwards. That was something that I did not have to think about; I did it unconsciously. At some point I fulfilled a dream of mine and bought some clipless pedals. With these pedals your foot fits snugly into the pedal, but the mechanism is completely different. Most importantly, you do not come out of the pedal when you pull your foot backwards, but rather when you turn it to the side. The first time I went riding in the neighborhood with the new pedals, I had to stop quickly at a stoplight. So, as I usually did, I came to a stop at the light, took my foot out of the pedal, and tried to put it on the ground for balance. But I couldn't get my foot out of the pedal. Then I realized that I had to turn it to the side instead of the way I unconsciously had done it, but not before I had already fallen down on the street. From then on, I reminded myself long before the next street light, that I had to take my foot out by moving it to the side. Sometimes I even pulled it out early. I also practiced in the same way while riding, taking my foot out from the side. Eventually I could do it automatically and I was amazed how much conscious effort I had to exert even with just to change a simple habit.

Scientists have found out that in familiar situations, we barely use our cerebrums. They have examined how active the brains of commuters are, when they take the daily trip to the office. They determined that almost only the brain stem is active, and that the cerebrum is turned off. Among other things, that can be very dangerous, because it is very hard for us to react quickly to dangerous situations.

Our body is always trying to save energy. It reduces the size of the muscles

which we do not use. It allows our nerve pathways to atrophy when we do not use them, which eventually causes us to lose intelligence. Industry has learned this, so at the moment there are a lot of so-called intelligence trainers for sale. Small computer games which through certain tasks attempt to make sure that our brain is used and trained. After you play these games for a while, the exercises also become a habit, which means that no new nerve pathways are created. Besides this, these games involve only a very small area of the brain. They are like machines in a gym, with which one can train just one muscle. To train the whole body, you either have to exercise on all kinds of machines, or do the kinds of sports which work the whole body. There are also sports which build up our coordination, balance, jumping power, etc. In everything we do we exert our muscles differently. In the same way, we should expose our brains to different influences, so that we can train them as universally as possible. And it is never too late.

Earlier, scientists thought that as one grows older, no new nerve pathways are formed. Since then, it has been discovered that it is possible to develop new nerve pathways when one is older. This means that we can stay mentally fit until we are old, or even become more mentally fit, as the years progress.

What do you think creates the most new nerve pathways and connections between the nerve pathways? Exactly. New learning, new behavior, new experiences, everything new. Fortunately we live in a world, where we will probably never be able to discover everything, so we can always learn, do, or experience something new.

The new connections in our brain allow us not only to have increased intelligence, but also an increased creativity and flexibility. We can suddenly think in directions in which we never before have thought. We can make the connections between things that we never thought had anything to do with each other. The possibilities that arise from this don't only help us in our careers, regardless of whether we are working for someone or for ourselves. They also make it easier for us to find solutions, maybe even unusual ones, in every part of our lives.

Also, when we are accustomed to always doing and experiencing new things, it becomes easier for us to deal with new situations. And not only that, if we are accustomed to doing something new, then we are also the first to adopt

new trends, even to start new ones. Can you imagine how your life would be, if you had been the first to be involved in the internet, and had founded Amazon or ebay? How about other megatrends, if you had been involved in them from the beginning? How would your life be now?

The times between new developments are always becoming shorter, so it is always more important to prepare your brain for the ever changing world. It is increasingly important to be open to new options as quickly as possible, and to recognize opportunities. It is increasingly important that you are constantly training your brain, not only on a machine, but as extensively and as much as possible, and in all areas. The comfort zone exercises in the practice part of the book can be a decisive step in this direction.

Change

Many people tend to change only when the stress and strain become too much. They become more and more unhappy with a situation, and at some point they realize that something must be changed, but just what is the question. Most people know exactly what they don't want any more in situations like these, but what do they want instead? So they don't really know what they want to change, and actually they wouldn't even really want to change, if only the situation weren't so uncomfortable. This is a horrible way to experience change, because it's more of a fight than it is fun.

There are also people, for whom change seems completely effortless, and for whom change is even fun. Interestingly, these people are always changing, sometimes in small, and sometimes in big steps. They decide when and what change they want, instead of waiting until there is just no other option.

So they have plenty of time to try out different alternatives, and chose the one that they think is best. And when one seems to be at a dead end, they find out later on that it was good at least to have given it a try. When they recognize that they are afraid to check out something new, they tackle it right away. They know the excuses that would hinder their progress, and they try uncomfortable alternatives that no one else tries. In doing this, they are many steps ahead of the rest of the world. They have their life in their hands, and they determine for themselves where it is going, instead of letting it push them around.

A good example of this is Madonna. Almost nobody would disagree that she is not the best singer, dancer, or actress, and that she doesn't conform to the classical ideal of beauty. But she has been successful in the music business for thirty years. She has also starred in films, and tried some other things. It has been said that her company is one of the fastest changing companies in the world. When you look at her career, you recognize that she has had no problem completely changing her style. She is always ready to try something new. Unfortunately I don't know how often she has tried something new, which we never found

out about, which was a personal development for her life. She has had a wide variety of experiences. She even tried out various religions, before choosing one.

Regardless of our motivation to change something, if it is too much psychological strain, or simply the desire for a better life, in the beginning there is always a decision to be made. Sometimes this decision is made for us, for example, when we are dismissed. There are some, though, that even then aren't willing to change. They keep going to work every day, or at least pretend to, instead of having to worry about another job, or finding another way to earn money. Fortunately those are isolated cases. But when a decision is made, what happens next? Where do you go from there? How do you know which direction is right? One thing is sure, that in order to change something, one must leave his comfort zone and do something new. At first it doesn't matter what, and in which direction. The most important thing is simply taking the first step. If you know where you want to go, then it is easier, and in the process it can be very wise to take an alternative route. But with the goal in sight, you can always see whether or not the steps you are taking are bringing you closer to the goal.

If you only know what you don't want, but not yet what you do want, then it is OK for you to experiment with many things. Go in one direction, then in another. Try to solve problems you have never attempted to solve. Try everything you can. Allow yourself to have as many experiences as possible, and observe yourself in the midst of them. Do whatever you enjoy. What makes you afraid? What bores you? The things that are boring, you can forget for now. Remember the things that are exciting for you. You should keep track of the ones you are afraid of. Why are you afraid of them? Is your life really endangered by them? How would it be if you weren't afraid?

Very often, our fears stand in the way of our development, and just beyond them is paradise. In order to really develop, we need to confront ourselves with our fears. Nowadays, unlike in times past, we can survive even though we take the easy road around challenges. But happiness is very often found on the other side of these challenges. But you can only

experience that when you try to take on the challenge at hand.

Have you overcome a few challenges? What did it do for your life? What did you enjoy about it? Can you see a pattern? You are now on your way to finding out what makes you really happy, and I can let you in on one secret, it is not the television. Maybe you manage to find a career on the way, maybe you will manage to recharge a bit in your free time. The first steps have been made, and every change begins with the first step, no matter how small.

Change and the Comfort Zone

In the many years in which I have been spending a lot of time dealing with the subject of change, one thing has become clear to me. Every change is ultimately leaving, or rather expanding one's comfort zone. It begins with the small things. Every change increases our possible courses of action. The ability which is most enhanced by comfort zone work is flexibility. That does not mean at all to be able to turn like a flag in the wind. Flexibility is the ability to quickly adjust oneself to one's surroundings. "Why should I adjust myself to my surroundings?" you might ask yourself. Basically it is simple. Flexibility determines your opportunities and your field of operation. The more flexible you are, the more alternatives are available for you.

Transformation und Initiation

In life we are always confronted with situations in which we stretch our comfort zones, by taking a step into a new stage in our lives. That begins at birth, coming out of the warm and protected environment of our mother's womb, where we don't have to worry about anything. Everything was taken care of. It was paradise. Suddenly we were confronted with a much colder world, in which we also had to take action to make sure that we had what we needed. In the beginning we could only do that through crying, in the hope that (mostly) our mother understood what we wanted. But over time we had to take care of ourselves more and more.

The next great expansion of our comfort zone was spending increasingly less time with mommy, or our parents. They were our caretakers, whom we trusted, but they also needed time for themselves, and so a babysitter took care of us once in a while. Then came preschool, and then school. The time spent with our parents diminished more and more, until we finally moved out, and stood on our own two feet. But we were always expanding our comfort zone on other levels. In the beginning we could only lay around and we had to be carried or pushed in a baby carriage. Over time we became more and more mobile. We learned how to turn ourselves over, and to move a few centimeters to the left or the right. Apart from that, our perception of our environment and our area of operation began to develop. At some point we began to crawl, and then to walk. Our world constantly became larger, and we could constantly explore more parts of that world. Using public transportation and the bicycle allowed us to explore our city and perhaps even nearby cities. After we had learned to do this once, we managed to do it alone, and decided for ourselves what we wanted to see. Soon we also learned to drive a car, to take the train, and get on an airplane. The world lay at our feet. Many people use all of these modes of transportation to travel around the world with a backpack, or at least to explore single countries and their inhabitants.

And what about our mental comfort zone, the boundaries within our

minds? In the beginning, we had to believe everything what our parents said. Later on we listened to a few more grownups, who wanted to tell us what was right and wrong. In school, we sometimes even had to repeat back the same information we had been given just to get good grades. Fortunately we were also taught how to formulate our own opinions, and to get information from all kinds of sources. The most important ability for this was reading. Before we could read, we had the radio, the television, and people around us, who influenced our opinions. With reading, all of the knowledge of the world was opened. In the meanwhile, internet became very easy to use, and full of information. But books and periodicals were easy for us to obtain. No matter what interested us, we could grapple the subject, and form our opinion. That was not always so. We should be aware of the possibilities and the responsibility that come with the increase of knowledge in our days.

The expansion of our comfort zone has also been coming about through our cultures for thousands of years. Amongst primitive people groups, there were so called rites of passage, which illustrated going from one phase of life to another. The young men amongst certain Native American tribes had to leave the village, and could only come back once they had slain an animal. For this it was necessary to be able to make one's own weapon, and be very skilled with its use. They had to read tracks, and be able to survive in the wild. They learned all of this in the preceding years, but they had never been sent out alone. When they came back with their slain prey, they were accepted into the group as men. Probably after this, they would never be sent out alone again, since they went hunting together most of the time. Today initiation rites take place in becoming a member of student unions, gangs, or religions, and other groups.

These rites differ greatly. With a religious group, they are mostly symbolic, with the candidates not being required to expand their comfort zone. In gangs and student unions they are more or less meaningful tests of courage or bond service where the candidate must prove that he really wants to belong to the group. In gangs, the tests of courage are mostly il-

legal activities, such as theft. The question is, whether the candidate really is tackling his fear by testing his courage, or is he just doing something crazy to prove his stupidity. There are plenty of opportunities to prove one's courage, without breaking the law. You will find some of them in the practice section of the book.

These tests of courage, especially popular among young men, were done earlier as initiations rites. Although we don't have these any more in the western world, it seems there is still a need for them. Earlier, the initiations rites were presided over by the older men in the tribe, who were wise and experienced. Today, those of the same age as those undergoing the initiations think them up and see that they are carried out accordingly. They themselves are still almost children, and can't know at all what will happen as a result. There is the great danger that these rituals are more harmful than useful. Young men want to prove themselves. They want to show that they are grownups. They draw a lot of self confidence from that. So we should give them boundaries for them to do this wisely, so that they grow up to become confident and intelligent young men. You will also find a few examples of these in the practice section. For the theme of childrearing, there are some very good books, a selection of which you can find in the literature section at www.komfortzonenbuch. de.

Since our lives began, we all have been more or less always occupied with expanding our comfort zones. Sometimes it occurs automatically, as with learning to walk. Sometimes we determine their expansion ourselves, when we decide what we want to try out, and sometimes it is determined from without, e.g., when we must go to school. In the beginning, our comfort zone is still very small, so we are always trying to stretch it. In time it develops into a size with which we can live. Then we are not so anxious to expand it. We believe that we know what holds our inner world together, what is right and what is wrong, what we like and what we don't like, etc. But this security is deceptive. Our fast-moving world cannot give us the security that tomorrow everything will be the same as it is today. From one day to the next everything can be different. To prepare for this, one must train one's ability to change.

If we regularly expand our world, experience unfamiliar things, and learn new things, then we gain our security from change instead of continuity. Benjamin Britten, a famous English composer, director and pianist, once said that "learning is like rowing against the current; once you stop, you drift back again." This has never been more true than it is today. We must be careful to apply this principle to our intellects, always feeding them with new knowledge. We must always be learning in every area. We have to take care of and train our bodies, because a strong and flexible body allows us to have a strong and flexible soul. We have to train our social conduct, our emotional intelligence, our creativity, our flexibility, and our openness. We have to confront our fears. All of these things can be achieved with the exercises in the practice part of the book.

The Hero's Journey

As I have been working with the subject change, I have noticed that large changes often follow a consistent pattern. I found that the conventional how-to-books have been of little use, most of them putting some new packaging around old wisdom. I finally discovered a book written in 1949 by Joseph Campbell. In "The Hero with a Thousand Faces," Campbell describes the "way of the hero." Campbell was in those times a well known mythologist, who investigated the origins of myths through the millennia. He investigated myths such as Buddha, Christ, Prometheus, Osiris, and many others, finding a common pattern in all of them. He named this the monomyth, which he described in his book. There are originally 12 steps contained in his book, but I reduced them to four points pertaining to change.

1. The Call to Adventure

First, the hero experiences some kind of a need or is given a task, either from someone else, or through a changed situation. He can choose to reject the task, and continue with his ordinary life, or accept the task and begin the journey of the hero. The decision is usually made reluctantly, as the hero must first muster up the confidence needed to take on the challenge. Once the decision is made, the journey into the unknown begins, where the hero goes beyond the realm of his own experience, and away from the conventions of society. In mythology, the hero's passage over the threshold into the underworld is also described.

2. The Road of Trials

Once the hero listens to the call of adventure, he is on the way confronted with various challenges. These challenges are successfully overcome, but can also be met with failure at the outset. The hero meets friendly and hostile figures on his way, which can also be seen as reflections of his own energy. Naturally the hostile figures stand in the way of the hero's overcoming the challenge, while the friendly figures help the hero to succeed and overcome great challenges.

3. The Ultimate Boon (reaching the goal)

At the end of his journey, the hero reaches his goal. In mythology, the hero often receives a treasure which can save the world- an elixir, or wisdom. These symbols represent the inner awareness which is connected with reaching the goal. In this way the transformation takes place. The hero hesitates to return to the everyday world, but he does return, having matured within.

4. Return

In his return to the everyday world, the hero is not understood by those around him. The insight which he has received by arriving at his goal is integrated and applied, and helps him to enrich his life in the normal world. This insight can also help to improve lives of others.

Joseph Campbell's book was never a bestseller, and he was little recognized in his lifetime. But many more recent stories are about the hero's journey. The film industry became alert to the significance of Campbell's work, when Christopher Vogler, a specialist for screenplays, wrote a book about his book. This book had great appeal amongst screen play writers in Hollywood, and countless films have drawn from the structure of the hero's journey, for example, George Lucas' Star Wars.

With reading this book you have already started your hero's journey. You have heard the call of adventure- now comes the time of trials.

Working with the Exercises

I have given a lot of thought to the selection of exercises in this book, and how they should be arranged. My goal was to arrange the exercises in such a way that someone can easily pass from one exercise to the next without noticing that they left their comfort zone long ago. Because everyone is different, I chose the order in such a way, that it was the easiest for the majority of those who tested the exercises.

Do the exercises in the order that they are given, if possible. If, in the meantime, one seems too hard for you, then continue on with the next ones. Take note of which exercise you skipped, and do it as soon as you feel ready for it. You should really do every exercise. As already mentioned in the introduction, it is helpful for you to observe yourself before, during, and after the exercise. For this, the following questions are useful:

*   How was I doing before the exercise? What was I thinking and feeling?

*   How was I doing during the exercise? What was I thinking and feeling?

*   How am I doing after the exercise? What am I thinking and feeling?

*   If I had to do the exercise again, how do I think I would think and feel then?

Do you recognize similarities amongst the individual exercises? Do you recognize a pattern in your behavior? Do you recognize strategies that you use to handle new situations?

By doing the exercises myself, I have recognized things such as how I behave, and above all, how I think, when I am afraid of something. My thoughts don't have anything to do with the situation directly, but they are always similar, whenever I sense fear. But these thoughts which I am confronted with also help me to notice that fear is present. So I can think about what could be troubling me, and then I can face the situation. In facing these situations, I have made some great steps in my own

www.comfortzonebook.com

personal development.

Do the exercises as they are described, and then try out the variations. Maybe you can also come up with some of your own variations.

With this kind of exercise, the experience of going through the exercise first-hand is crucial. You can't always logically deduce what an exercise will achieve for you. That's what makes life interesting- you never know what will come next.

It is up to you whether you decide to do these exercises.

THE EXERCISES

1 Contact with others

Contact with others is a basic ability needed for an enjoyable life, so we will start off with a large assortment of related exercises.

1.1 Eye Of The Tiger!

Communication takes place at many levels. There is verbal and nonverbal communication. Many people are not aware that it is nonverbal communication that has greater meaning. Like when you first meet someone, and you know right away whether they are friendly or not. You can tell, without them saying a word.

Although nonverbal communication is so important, our communication is more and more limited to verbal communication, because we are using more and more technical means of communication. Over the telephone or mobile phone, only the voice can be transmitted, at least until now. At least the nonverbal components such as tone, rate of speaking, and so on, are preserved. In e-mails or in chatting, even this information is lost, and smileys and cryptic abbreviations are used in an attempt to replace it. Apparently, nonverbal communication is still important, despite how much we use technology. As the old saying, "The eyes are the windows of the soul," brings out, the eyes have a very important place in our nonverbal communication. What is even more incredible is that more and more people do not look at each other. It seems they are afraid to look at someone in the eyes, perhaps even because they don't want the other person to see too closely what is going on inside of them. There are also people, who seek eye contact, and keep it, not in a pushy way, but who look interested. These people are mostly people who seem to have charisma. With such people, we feel that we are being noticed and understood.

Task:

Look people in the eye, whether it is your conversation partner, or someone who walks by you on the street. Learn to keep eye contact, and observe their facial expression, after the other person has broken eye contact. You learn the most when you seek out eye contact with those who you think have charisma. Try to develop a feeling for the right look: don't stare, and blink from time to time. Find a kind word to say, if someone speaks to you.

Do this exercise for at least 4 weeks.

Variations:

*   While you are looking people in the eye, think about different things. Look at it as a competition for who can keep eye contact the longest.

*   Some other time, overwhelm someone you meet with sincere compliments, or think badly about them. Then notice what this does for you, the other person, and your contact with one another.

1.2 Just smile!

In the cultural context of the western world, seriousness is an important principle. In Asia, this is the other way around. There people smile a lot more. Smiling is not limited to the first time you meet, but people smile in nearly every situation.

If you've ever seen an Asian person with a grin on his face at 35°C, while he is pushing his moped because he ran out of gas, then you know what I mean.

No one can resist a smile. In psychology, it has been long recognized that smiling has many benefits for the psyche.

Take care when doing the exercise, that you have a smile that really comes from inside, and isn't just put on.

Task:

For the next four weeks, smile genuinely at all of the people you meet. These smiles should come from within. Observe the effect that this has on the other person, and their reaction. Use a smile in seemingly difficult situations that come up in your job or in your everyday life.

Variationen:

- Seek contact with people, to whom you have always been afraid to come close, and smile at them.

- Also smile while you are on the phone.

www.comfortzonebook.com

1.3 Call me!

In the course of your life, you probably have gotten to know and to appreciate many people who have accompanied you on life's way. You have probably more or less lost touch with some of them.

Many times it is sheer laziness that keeps us from reviving some of our old contacts. So the joy is even greater, when you take the effort to reconnect and talk with some old friends about old times. And this is also a great way to see where one has come in life.

Your life is defined by its different parts, such as school, studies, and career. Have you ever noticed that you have gotten to know different people in every part of your life? The more flexible that you are to integrate people and experiences from the various parts of your life into your present day life, the more variety your life can have.

Task:

Make yourself a list of friends whom you have known for a long time, but have not had contact with for while. And make sure to include all the parts of your life (school, college, and career). Call at least ten of them and arrange meetings with them.

Variations:

*   Make an "Old School" party with your old friends.

*   Do the same with old classmates.

1.4   Write Letters!

Communication between people is one way we express our appreciation for each other. Today, communication has greatly changed because of technology. We can send e-mails, chat, call via internet, write an SMS, or call with a mobile phone or land line. Communication has become faster and easier, but it has also become much more transient, and is also very often reduced. Composing a hand written letter requires time, but it has many advantages. You make what you have to say more personal, and you give more thought to what you really want to convey. And I have never met anyone who isn't glad to receive a handwritten letter.

Task:

Write hand written letters to some of your important communication partners, and take your time in doing so.

Variations:

• Write postcards from places that you visit.

• Write with different kinds of pens. Use a fountain pen, a ball point pen, or even a feather pen, if you have one.

• Write a nice story for someone on a post card, and send them the next part every few days.

www.comfortzonebook.com

1.5   Change your Style!

Every one of us, consciously or unconsciously, displays something about their inner life in the way that they dress. Do you know what impact you make with what you wear? I think it is a good idea to get outside advice about this. In clothing shops, you will find your own free style specialist, who specializes in this field. What could be better than having one of them give you advice?

Once you have done this a few times, you will have learned a lot about yourself and about good style. Maybe you will also learn how you can dress advantageously in different situations, and what impact this can have on those around you. But just remember that in the end it is all a matter of opinion, and that you have every right to have your own style.

Task:

Next time you go shopping for clothes ask the sales person to give you some advice. First choose someone who you think is nice, and then pick someone who you don't think is nice. Have them give you as much advice as they are willing to give, and try out different styles. Which style fits you best in which situations and why? Find out which clothing brings out which positive sides of you, and how.

Variations:

*   Go into stores where you have never been, or which at first glance don't seem to go with your current style.

*   Go into stores with different price ranges, from very cheap, to very expensive.

*   Do the same thing when you buy shoes or go to the hair dresser.

1.6   Welcome to the Neighbourhood!

Up until now, I have moved around a lot. I can still remember my childhood, which I spent in a small town. I lived almost the entire time there in one house, and got to know all of the children in the area, and spent a lot of time with them. Since then I have moved into a new neighborhood 7-8 times, and every time I have been confronted with the task of finding my way around.

Until now, I have always used the opportunity of moving in to introduce myself personally to my neighbors. In doing so, I have had some enjoyable experiences, and have never once met with a negative response. It was very surprising for me to find out, after asking around amongst my acquaintances, that many of them did not know their closest neighbors, and they did not introduce themselves when they moved in. In the big cities, it seems more and more the trend to live anonymously.

Task:

In the next two weeks, get to know your closest neighbors, in case you don't already. If you already know the ones in your own apartment building, use this exercise as an opportunity to explore the nearby area.

Variations:

* Host a house party, to which you invite all of your neighbors, or that you organize together.

* In case you have lived in the same place for a long time, get to know people a little further away from you, like in local businesses, sports clubs, etc.

www.comfortzonebook.com

1.7   Giving Compliments!

It always seems strange to me how easy it is for many people to disturb, to blame, or even to curse someone else. For many, having trouble giving or receiving compliments has become practically the norm. Few people even know how you can give a compliment at all. And it only occurs to a few why they should even consider complimenting anyone in the first place.

Several steps are necessary to make compliments. First you have to really observe the other person carefully. What do you notice about them? Where have they really made an effort to, for example, really look good? Which beliefs have an influence on their world, which through a well placed compliment could be weakened or strengthened? To train your attentiveness, you can also use Exercise 1.15.

Through this exercise, you direct your attention towards the positive things about another person, and in doing so you make your own world even more positive. In the Hawaiian language, there is a proverb, "Energy flows where attention goes." Where are you directing your energy?

Task:

For four weeks, give sincere compliments to your fellow men.

Variations:

*   Give at least 5 (10, 20…) sincere compliments a day.

*   Give compliments to strangers on the street, at the supermarket, etc.

1.8   Be interesting and interested!

Have you ever met someone, whose words you hung upon when you are listening to them, to whom you could have listened to forever? Do you also know people, around whom you let down your guard and tell them all about yourself, although you might have just met them? You have the feeling that they are interested in you and what you have to say. You can learn to be both- an interested and an interesting person.

We have all experienced things in life that make us unique. Most of us are just not aware what they are. So sometimes it is hard for people to find themselves interesting, which is one prerequisite for being an inte-resting person. Despite this, you have also met people who find them-selves very interesting, whom you find boring, whose company you want to escape as quickly as possible. So being interesting is not just about finding yourself interesting. You also have to be interested. Only when you are interested in another person can you tell whether or not he is interested in what you are telling him. Be perceptive and change the way that you speak, and what you say, until you notice real interest. You will soon realize that there are things that always work, and others that only work in specific situations. You have already learned one of the abilities that practically always work in Exercise 1.1. Exercise 1.2 is also very helpful.

Task:

Through interesting conversation topics, make sure that your conversa-tion partner gladly speaks with you for a long time. Two hours is a good amount of time for a conversation about deeper things. Be an interesting conversation partner, and then be the conversation partner who is more interested in the other. Develop a balance between your presentation, and expressing interest in your conversation partner.

www.comfortzonebook.com

Variations:

- Also have such conversations with charismatic people.

- Practice the same thing on the telephone

- Tell children stories so that they listen gladly and attentively.

1.9 Call the Devil!

Who isn't familiar with this? An uncomfortable call can be put off for days, and one always seems to find other tasks to do that are supposedly more important. Whether it is the call to the tax office, a special client, a supplier, the boss, or following up leads…

I know one case where a friend of mine put off 25 calls to customers. It was never the right day, or there was never enough time, or there were too many distractions. At some point there were so many calls to make, that she had to reserve an entire day for them. It was very interesting, that after she took care of the 25 calls, she would have gladly made another 25 calls right away. She went home with a very positive feeling. By the way, that was the last time that she ever put off making a phone call.

Sometimes instead of taking care of something, an avoidance strategy comes into play. But this avoidance strategy doesn't have take place at all. The faster the call is taken care of, the faster your head is free for important things. For me, I used avoid doing uncomfortable things by adding many other activities into my schedule that had to be done at some point, but really could have been easily put off until later.

There is a simple rule: as soon as you discover the smallest sign of uneasiness, make the call right then and there. Try to make as many calls as you can. The more you practice ridding yourself of this uneasiness by taking action, the more that this behavior will also be carried over into other situations, and will make you a more active person.

When making these calls, always think about Exercise 1.2. Smile.

Task:

Make a list of all the calls that you are supposed to take care of, or have put off for a while. Phone the list right away and feel good about it.

Variationen:

- What is uncomfortable for you to do? Make a list, and do those things.

- Whenever tasks make you feel uneasy, do them right away.

1.10 Cooking Group!

There are increasingly few people who enjoy cooking. Processed food is more and more a part of our lives. Besides, we eat more and more often alone, although sometimes we do eat together with our families. When we eat with friends, we go out most of the time. But it is so much fun to cook together-conversing and learning cooking tricks from each other, and then enjoying the product of the work together.

Many times it is much more comfortable at home than in a restaurant, and when everyone works together, a meal can be made quickly and easily.

Task:

Once a month or more often, organize a cooking event together with friends, acquaintances, or even strangers. Give some thought beforehand to what you want to cook, and who cooks what. Coordinate a menu together. Cook in a new style in which you never have cooked, or make something you never have eaten.

Variations:

• After the meal, play a game together.

• Have a theme for each evening, like Thai cuisine.

www.comfortzonebook.com

1.11 No Hands, please...!

Have you ever noticed that a lot of parties more or less take place in the kitchen? Then why not make the meal something extraordinary and give the party some zip?

For shy people, by the way, this is a very good opportunity to meet people in a different way. Either they speak with others, or they go hungry for the night.

Task:

Organize a party where the guests are not allowed to eat with their own hands. Decide for yourself whether you announce this beforehand or not.

Variations:

*   You are only allowed to be fed once by each guest, so that each guest has to speak with everyone.

*   The food is only given after a certain task is fulfilled, such as the person who is to be fed introducing themselves in an interesting way or telling an interesting story from their lives.

*   Don't let the guests use any silverware.

*   The guests are only allowed to use the weaker hand when feeding each other.

1.12 Hug people!

In the age of the internet, with communication taking place by e-mail/chatting/SMS, direct contact with other people is becoming less and less.

Meanwhile, a well known video on You Tube, called the Free Hug Campaign shows another option.

The first challenge is to go around in a busy area with a sign which says, "Free hugs." Then, you have to motivate people to hug you, allowing physical closeness. If people come to you on their own, then by all means, hug them heartily and joyfully, no matter who it is. The icing on the cake is when you give other people signs at the end too, which normally is supposed to lead to a hugging "epidemic."

Task:

Make several signs with the title, "Free Hugs," in at least A3 format. Then glue them to pieces of cardboard, and off you go. Go to a busy area like a shopping street, shopping center, or a similar place, and gather as many hugs as possible. Motivate other people to hug you, which can take a while in the beginning, but after a while it becomes easier. Give out signs to other adventurous people, who want to have the same kind of fun themselves.

Variations:

*   Invent your own variations that are suitable for your surroundings (business, party, etc.).

1.13 Stand up and fight!

It is difficult for many people to express and to defend their opinions in an argument or a similar situation. Unfortunately, because of this a lot of knowledge and experience cannot be used to their full potential.

A very intelligent colleague of mine had just this problem. He sat in meetings with his head full of good ideas, but unfortunately he lacked the confidence to express them aloud. Fortunately he confided in me after the meeting, so that we could actually use some of his ideas. Over time, I realized how good his ideas really were.

If this sounds familiar to you, then it is even more important for you to do the following exercise. Additionally, you will educate yourself in rhetoric, and you might even become more charismatic.

Task:

Find someone with whom you can discuss something. Prepare yourselves to discuss a theme, where one stands for one side and your friend the other side. If you feel confident, be bolder and start to express your opinion in meetings, conversations, arguments, family debates, etc. Convince those around you with your arguments, but be careful not to overwhelm them.

Variations:

*   Join a debate club

*   At election time, address the representatives of a certain political party, who stand out on the street corner talking to people, and have a discussion with him.

*   Express your opinion in forums, blogs, and social networks on the internet.

1.14 Talk and listen!

I am always meeting people for whom it is hard to ask a stranger for directions or for the time. But these are great opportunities to speak with and get to know interesting people.

I once read in a book that said that everyone that crosses our path has a message for us. But to receive this message we have to speak with or address them. In the beginning this was very hard for me, but eventually I found out that the book was right. And even more fascinating is the fact that every person is unique, and that we can learn something from everyone, directly or indirectly.

If you attempt to do this exercise, you won't only get to know people better, how they think and feel, but you will also always come across ideas that will bring you forward in your current situation in life. You will recognize how interesting and inspiring the perspectives of others can be, and I am sure that you will integrate one or the other into your own life.

Task:

Speak with strangers everywhere.

Variations:

*   Speak with strangers, whom you meet again and again, for example every morning on the subway.

*   Speak with strangers who seem friendly to you, perhaps after you have done exercise 1.1 or 1.2.

*   Interview strangers. Ask them what they are thinking about at the moment, and what they think and feel. Ask them about important experiences in their lives, and how these experiences changed them. Ask them about their opinions about whatever spontaneously occurs to you. Think up some more topics, and conduct interviews on them.

www.comfortzonebook.com

1.15 Pop Star!

One of the most important aspects of communication is your attentiveness for the other party. Everyone loves it when someone recognizes that they have a new haircut, some nice new pants, or some other positive change.

Attentiveness can be taught. You can learn to be attentive by doing certain exercises. You will find some examples here.

Task:

Make a big bag of popcorn for yourself. Take one piece out and observe it carefully. Take a picture of it from all sides, and stick it back into the bag. Shake it, so that you can't see it anymore, and begin to look for this same piece. Once you think you have found it, compare it with the photos you took. Do this exercise as often as it takes for you to easily relocate the popcorn.

Variations:

*   Ask a friend or acquaintance of yours to travel the same route as you go to work, and to take pictures of spots that stand out. Have them show you the pictures they have taken, and find out where each one was taken. First have them take pictures of bigger things like houses or intersections, and once that works well have them photograph smaller and smaller things. My girlfriend, for example, after doing this exercise, realized for the first time that there is a public toilet on the main road she had been taking every day for a few months.

- Draw or describe a room in your apartment as accurately as possible.

- When you are walking on your way somewhere with a friend, and you pass by someone, each of you tries to describe them. What they had on, which hair color they had, which eye color they had, etc. Describe them as accurately as possible.

- Come up with your own exercises for you to train your attentiveness.

www.comfortzonebook.com

1.16 E-mail for you!

Personal ads exist in various forms. There are more ways to use this form communication than just looking for a partner. For example, when you are looking for a sport partner, someone to go somewhere with, to make music together with, or just get to know someone new, then personal ads work quite well.

The goal of this exercise is to acquaint you with many ways of getting in touch with people. In exercise 1.8 you learned how you can be interesting for other people. Use those abilities in this exercise. The more often you connect with people in this way, the more experienced you will be in using this method, and the easier it will be for you to convey a personal touch in e-mails.

Task:

Put up a personal ad, and wait and see what kind of feedback you get. Make sure when you write it that you address the audience you intend to reach.

Variations:

- Use various internet portals such as www.new-in-town.de, www. kijiji.de, www.twotickets.de, www.single.de, and so forth.

- Answer personal ads.

1.17 Lonely People!

If you have ever been in the hospital, you know perhaps that it can be a very lonely place. Some people are fortunate to be visited often. But what about those which are not so fortunate?

In many studies it has been determined that positive emotions help to speed up the recovery process. Today there are even clowns that are sent to patients, especially to children. But not only clowns can make a patient feel good- you can do so just as well.

Task:

Visit a stranger in the hospital or nursing home, and bring them flowers or some other present. Do this for a few weeks once a week. Ask the nurses or caretakers to tell you who hasn't gotten a lot of visits, or has no nearby family. Visit them, converse with them, and cheer them up.

Variations:

* Have them talk about the best times of their lives.

* Ask them to tell their life story.

* Play with children in a nursery, or in a children's home.

1.18 Get in Touch!

Most people never give too much thought to the subject of touch, although it is very important for our well being. Every one of us comes into the world with various needs, one of which is the need for touch and body contact. Although physical contact is so important, some people are reluctant to allow it. Touching is only one aspect of a cuddle party. At a cuddle party, you also learn how to deal with the word "no." At a cuddle party everyone is only allowed to do that which they are given permission to do. If someone doesn't want to cuddle with you, then they will make that unmistakably clear to you. You'll discover very quickly that is nothing against you personally. Also, at a cuddle party you have the opportunity to get to know many new people in a totally new way. You are physically close before you have the opportunity to have a verbal exchange.

Task:

Go to a cuddle party!

Variationen:

• Organize your own cuddle party.

• Organize a massage party.

1.19 Get Rich!

In America there is the story of the dishwasher who becomes a millionaire. In Germany, in the past few years more and more people want
to become millionaires from matches, as some Americans have already
managed to do. I wasn't out to become a millionaire from a matchstick,
but I have done the exercise several times. My best result was that after
two hours, I had come back with a new scooter worth 120 Euros. That is
quite an increase in value, huh?

This exercise is about speaking to people and developing good salesmanship and negotiating skills.

Task:

Take a match or a toothpick and trade it with someone for something
worth a bit more. Take that and trade it again. Trade as long as you like,
provided you trade for at least two hours, and trade at least 25 times.

Variation:

•   Trade to reach a predetermined goal.

1.20 It's Play Time!

In restaurants, cafes, and so on, all kinds of people meet with one another, and seclude themselves as though they really were alone. You would think that there were invisible walls between the tables. Whenever I pay close attention, I always seem to recognize that those sitting at a neighboring table seem to be very interesting people, at least as far as I can tell from their conversations. I have often caught myself wanting to join in the conversation, or ask about a particular detail of it.

It sometimes seems to me, that other guests feel the same way. The following exercise makes it much easier to break the ice and to make interesting contacts.

This exercise creates common ground for speaking with someone you don't know through playing a game. Also, the time which is spent together with the other people might be longer than the game, if not just as long. Or else it is as long as you are able to keep an interesting conversation going.

Task:

Make a sign with the inscription: "Play with me (or us)!" Take the sign and a few board games and go into the locale of your choice that is at least half full. Put the sign and the game on the table. If no one reacts to your sign, speak with them and invite them to play with you. Make the game interesting for them.

Variations:

*   Play in an airplane or in a train with other travel guests.

*   Play with coworkers on lunch break.

*   In addition to the game and the sign, pack a camping table and some camping chairs with you, and set them up in a shopping center, public swimming pool, or other busy place.

1.21 Random Acts of Kindness!

Time and time again there are moments in life, where one can make an amazing impression on someone with just the smallest act of kindness. What is it worth to you to make a lasting impression on someone in a short amount of time? With me, it started in line at the grocery store. An older woman was in front of me, who came one euro short of being able to pay her bill. I spontaneously gave her a euro, and she wouldn't stop thanking me. Not everyone is so open to receiving unexpected gifts. Time and time again I have tried to take the bill for other people in line, at the bakery, at the kiosk, etc., meeting with all kinds of results, but you will find this out for yourself soon enough...

In my opinion, the nicest experience you can have with this exercise is putting a smile on someone's face. Another interesting thing to notice is how people handle receiving gifts, and how often they put up their defenses, when someone just wants to be kind to them.

Task:

Pay the bill for strangers. Things like bread at the bakery, newspapers, or a coffee are quite enough. You have the advantage that no one anticipates this random act of kindness. Pay attention to the amount that the person in front of you has to pay, and determine whether this amount isn't too much, and then just pay for them.

Variation:

*   Let them know beforehand that it's your treat..

1.22 It's Party Time!

Now that you have completed all of the exercises in the first chapter, you have earned a party. Naturally not a normal party, but a party that's in the spirit of this book.

What is the coolest thing about a party? Getting to know new people, right? Then how about a party with only new people? But you have the right to invite and get to know only the people that seem at first glance to be nice people. Well, this should be easy. Let's get to it!

This exercise is especially good for people who have recently moved into a new city.

Task:

Design an invitation and give it out to strangers that you meet, whom you would like to have come to your party. Depending on your budget, you can determine what you serve and what the guests bring. Perhaps you serve the drinks, and ask your unknown guests to bring the snacks.

Variations:

*   Have a theme for the party.

*   Do the party as described in exercise 1.11.

*   Announce the party on sites like www.couchsurfing.org, etc.

www.comfortzonebook.com

2 Breaking the Routine

Everyone is familiar with the hamster that is forever running and going nowhere inside a wheel. Routine is not necessarily negative; sometimes it offers a form of security, as is the case with rituals like starting the day of work with a cup of coffee.

It has been proven by brain researchers that routine and always having the same daily schedule leave the brain unfit. Just as it is important for our bodies and muscles that we use them, it is also important for our brains. The best way to give the brain mental training is to organize our activities with plenty of variety.

From the standpoint of neurochemistry, it is completely OK if in the first fifteen minutes of your day, you don't do everything differently than usual. But after this time, your brain is up to operating temperature, so it is thankful for anything new.

In the next pages you will find the optimal workout routine for your brain.

2.1   Use the Other One!

Everyone has one hand which they prefer, with which they do their everyday activities. Recently it has become commonly known that each hand is connected with the opposite side of the brain. So there are certain exercises for the whole brain, called cross-over exercises, which have the goal of stimulating both sides of the brain. But it is also possible to accomplish the same thing in a simpler and more interesting way.

For example, I first started to eat with chopsticks with my strong hand, and then I changed to my weaker hand. Surprisingly, my weak hand was much better at using the chopsticks than the strong one. In addition to better stimulating and connecting the two sides of the brain, you also become more aware of your everyday activities. You interrupt the automatic behavior of your daily routine and turn your attention to the things that you are doing at the moment. It is also an easy opportunity to teach your brain something new.

Task:

Use your weaker hand for your daily activities such as writing, brushing your teeth, eating, shaving, showering, applying lotion, using the mouse, and so on, until they feel comfortable for you.

www.comfortzonebook.com

2.2   Get up!

Maybe you have seen the movie, Groundhog Day, with Bill Murray. Well, does your morning always seem to be the same? Do you organize your morning consciously or are you a slave of your habits? Then it is now time to start your day with a purpose and take life into your own hands early in the morning. I was one of those people who could spend hours in bed after the alarm went off, before deciding to get up. In my opinion that is not the best way to start the day, first of all because the whole time I would be thinking how I didn't want to get up. Maybe it has been the same for you. At some point I read about an Indian breathing technique, which changed the start of my day completely. Now, I jump out of bed in the morning full of energy. This exercise, along with helping you to break out of your routine, allows you to find your optimal morning schedule. If you manage to change every morning, then you change your days as well.

Task:

Get up and begin your day differently than you began yesterday. Perhaps you change your thoughts before you even open your eyes. Or you breathe deeply ten times and flood your body and your brain with oxygen and energy. Then, when you shower, do so with cold water, as Kneipp suggested (Kneipp was a famous German who studied natural remedies and specialized in hydrotherapy). Then sit down in a different place than usual and consciously notice the new perspective. What do you normally listen to in the morning? Listen to something completely different, like a nice audio-book, another style of music, or nothing, for a change. Read another newspaper, or don't read one at all.

Variations:

*   What can you change about your morning? Put together a list of possibilities and try them out.

*   Talk with friends, colleagues, acquaintances about how they start their days, and begin yours in the same way.

2.3 Take the Other Way!

With the preceding exercise, you have successfully changed your morning. Now you can devote yourself to making your way to work just as creative.

A friend of mine once decided that instead of driving to the office, he would take the train for a while. His first time on the train, a young lady got into the same car as him a few stations after he did, and she seemed to him to be a very nice girl. After taking the train a few more times, he took his chances and decided to speak with her, and they became a couple. In this way the decision to make a small change in his routine changed his life.

This exercise is connected with the preceding one, and should be done at the same time.

Task:

Every day, find a new way to work or take a different mode of transportation. If you normally go by car, take the public or your bike, even if it takes a bit longer. Always go different ways. Park your car somewhere else. Leave for work at a different time.

Variations:

• Find the nicest, the fastest, and the most interesting ways to work.

• To other destinations, take different routes than the ones you are familiar with.

2.4 Hopping around!

Since you have already made changes to your morning and your route to work, it is time to do another new thing on top of that.

Have you ever noticed that different places put you in different moods? I have found a place where I am truly creative. Other places make me feel very relaxed. Every place has a certain atmosphere, which you experience with your senses. Everywhere you go you can find different smells, sounds, and other impressions.

Task:

Visit places where you never were- whether they are buildings, places or streets in your home town, or another city. Observe what effect each place has on you.

Variations:

• Find places that give you strength or help you rest, or have a good effect on you in some way. Make a list of these places and visit them. Then when you need rest, for example, go to the place on your list that helps you to rest.

2.5 Moving around!

Most of us spend a lot of time in our apartments, and once they are arranged, most of us don't rearrange them very often at all. Amongst the Chinese, it has long been recognized that the position of the furniture and other fixtures has an effect upon our lives. They bring together all of the science behind this under the name Feng Shui. Even if you don't believe in this, you can most likely imagine that something changes when you change the position of the furniture in the apartment. Whenever I straighten up, I can see right away an increase in my productivity. I witnessed the results of this when I completely rearranged my work room. Suddenly I got some innovative ideas for some of my projects. Somehow my perspective, in the truest sense of the word, had changed.

You too have the opportunity to take in new perspectives and to see what a rearranged apartment does for your life, and whether the Chinese aren't really on to something with their Feng Shui.

Task:

Rearrange your apartment. Perhaps at first you just decorate it, or you can start right off moving the furniture around.

Variations:

*   Clean out your closets and put everything back in. Get rid of what you don't need. How you can do this is described in Exercise 2.13.

*   Rearrange your work area.

*   Rearrange your apartment again as soon as the change you just made starts to feel comfortable for you.

2.6   Change your Brain Food!

In Germany alone, there are well over 6,000 periodicals, and apparently there are also people who read them. How many of these do you know and a how many do you read?

Just a little while ago I browsed through the periodicals in the central railway station, and although the magazine stores there have a very large selection, this is only a small percentage of all of those that exist. Nevertheless, the magazines in such big stores are very well sorted by topic, so I could quickly get an overview of them. Even for subjects which I normally am quite familiar with, there were to my amazement magazines that had different layouts and styles of writing, often containing completely new perspectives. Much more instructional were the magazines about other subjects, some of which I had never seen before, or at least had never taken any interest in. The world looks different to everyone. There is no such thing as the one true reality. The more that you interchange with people with different views of life, the larger your own world will become, along with your comfort zone.

Task:

Go to a large newspaper kiosk at least once a week, buy and read a newspaper or magazine that you have never read before. When you are finished, go online and browse through an even richer variety of information.

Variations:

*   Read theses about topics that interest you, and then read about themes that you might never have heard of.

*   Read books that cover themes unfamiliar to you or genres you previously held for uninteresting.

*   Go online to www.ted.com or www.poptech.org and take a look at how other people imagine the future.

2.7   Everybody Dance Now!

We all have our own favorite music genres, favorite clubs and favorite radio stations. For example, I am definitely not a fan of heavy metal. Even so, a long time ago a friend of mine convinced me to go with her to a heavy metal club. How can I describe it? I had a really nice night and I was surprised and impressed by the sort of people that were there. Pretty much every kind of person was represented, from business-types to rockers, and everyone was in a good mood. Heavy metal is still not my kind of music, but since then I go to a Heavy Metal club now and then and enjoy a totally different world.

So you already listen to heavy metal? Then try out a techno club! So you love rap music? Then go to a Gothic concert! So far you only know the philharmonic as a place of interest? Then go on in! In completing this exercise you might feel uncomfortable at first. The more you get used to the new sound and get to know the people, the more fun and opportunities you'll have.

Task:

Make yourself a list of different styles of music, and then find opportunities to become acquainted with them. Maybe go to a classical concert, an opera, a punk party, or a techno club.

Variationen:

*   Go alone to a club where you never have gone, and meet new people.

*   Change your radio station regularly.

*   Go to music festival where they play a music style that is new for you. www.festivals.com

www.comfortzonebook.com

2.8   Silence, please!

In Germany it used to be common that one did not speak while eating. In our hectic day and age however, mealtime has become the only time for conversations. In this way we give ourselves the chance to enjoy the food and to give our discussion partner our complete attention. What would happen, if we split the two activities and scheduled one time only to eat, and another time only to converse?

Task:

For one week, eat without talking. Set aside a special time to have the conversation that you left out, this time on purpose, not just haphazardly.

Variations:

- Do exactly the opposite- eat while watching TV, while reading the newspaper, or speaking with someone else. Compare that with the exercise above.

- Eat twice as slowly.

- Chew every bite at least 30 times.

- After every bite, say, "Mmm," in your head or out loud.

2.9 Change your Diet!

Everywhere you read about how some foods are supposedly healthy and how some aren't. It's funny that you read in one place that one food is healthy, and in another place that it isn't. Who is right then? Perhaps both are right, only for different groups of people. So it is up to you to find out what is good for you and what isn't.

I don't want to be a diet policeman and try to get you to start eating healthy, even though it is clearly a good choice. I am talking about changing your habits, and what you eat is one thing in your day that regularly repeats. But you can change the way that this repetition takes place.

Task:

If you are eating completely healthy at the moment, then eat something unhealthy. If you are eating unhealthy, then eat healthy for a full month. In doing so, find what is good for you and what isn't.

Variations:

- Change how often and when you eat.

- Read nutritional guides and try out the advice they give.

- Every week, cook something you have never cooked before.

www.comfortzonebook.com

2.10 Treat Yourself!

You hear from a lot of people that they have never been to a fancy restaurant. Some think that they wouldn't feel comfortable in one, maybe because they are not used to being around high society. Do these people want to. But why should you rob yourself of an opportunity like this, just because of what you assume that people would think?

There are others who say that they don't want to pay so much money for a meal. Whatever the reasons against it might be, the experience of treating yourself to something really good is definitely worth it. Look in gourmet guides like Michelin, or search online for excellent restaurants nearby.

Task:

Reserve a good table in a really good restaurant. Ask the waiter what the specialty of the house is. Ask the wine steward which wine goes best with each course. Observe and taste the difference between that and your normal food. Enjoy the food and feel at home.

Variations:

- Use your best silverware every time you eat.

- Also, treat yourself to something good in other culinary areas, like an expensive wine, white tea, a special coffee, etc. (Go against the mentality that cheaper is better).

2.11 Information Diet!

Did you ever notice how much time most people spend exposing themselves to the different media? TV, radio, newspaper, internet, telephone- and the list goes on. If you ask them what they consider important or what they have gotten out of this influx of information, then you can see just how much time has been wasted, and how little there is to show for it.

A while ago I was in Egypt, and for six days I was in the desert. I didn't hear anything about world events. I just enjoyed the quiet. Mobile phones and radios didn't work, there was no daily newspaper, and of course no TV. Believe it or not, I was despite of this, or perhaps because of this, happy, and I began to enjoy this silence even more. I had a lot of time to occupy myself with those around me. A few months ago I had already gotten rid of the TV at home, and my evenings completely changed. Earlier on, I had eaten in front of the TV, so no real conversations could develop.

Through this exercise you will become more aware of what is really important for you, and what's just adding to the noise around you.

Task:

For one week, abstain from every media- TV, radio, newspaper, mp3-player, books, and of course the internet. No more e-mails. Use the time you normally devote to them to an active occupation like sports, conversations, meetings with friends, etc.

Variations:

Go without using your telephone and your mobile phone- that means don't write any SMS's.

2.12 The Bucket List!

The movie The Bucket List is about two terminally ill men and how they find a lust for life again. The bucket list is a list with all of the things that one wants to do in their life.

Most of us have a plan that we would like to attain in our lives, but it is only in our heads. So these things remain vague, and the chances that they could ever really happen diminish in time. Something more concrete, like a written list, helps you to plan on doing these things right away, then to carry them out, and finally to lead the life that you actually want to lead.

This exercise is about discovering your goals for your life and realizing how you can reach them.

Task:

Make a list with things that you would like to have, do, or be, at first with at least 100 entries. Sort them by priority and make the first steps to being able to cross off the first five entries.

Variations:

• Give yourself a certain amount of time for the five most important things on your list.

• Add the exercises in this book to your list of goals.

2.13 Let it go!

In the course of time most people collect all sorts of more or less useful things. When moving, you realize just how many of them you have, when the number of moving box seems infinite and everything still isn't packed.

I became aware of this while reading a book. I had just finished reading a few pages, and I was just dying to do something about all of my junk. I wanted to get rid of stuff, and that is unusual for me. I went on a cleaning spree, and I sorted my whole apartment. It resulted in a carload of "junk"- all of the stuff I had collected through the years, and didn't need, but was too good to throw away. Thank goodness for e-Bay, so that nowadays you don't have to throw away things like nice gifts from family. If you are interested, you can find that book in the book list on www.komfortzonenbuch.de.

There is a psychological dead weight attached to things that aren't taken care of. As soon as you throw away the things that you don't need, the corresponding attachment in your mind is resolved. At the same time you learn a simple way of letting go of something...

Task:

Rid yourself of all of the things you don't need. In case you aren't sure how to tell what you don't need, it's simple. If you haven't used it in the last 12 months, you don't need it. Most importantly, remember the things that are in the basement, on your rooftop terrace, in your shed, or hidden away someplace.

Variations:

*   Sell the items you set aside at a flea market or on Ebay or Craigslist.

www.comfortzonebook.com

2.14 Speed Reading!

As we have already seen in the preceding exercises, we have the luck or the misfortune of having access to an as good as infinite amount of information. To become free of all of this information, as you read about in exercise 2.11, is not always the ideal solution. But it does help to find out which pieces of information are important and which aren't. If you know which pieces of information are important to you, whether for your career or for your private life, then it also makes sense to be able to access the information as quickly as possible. The process of retrieving the information should be as quick as possible, so that you have more time to apply what you learn.

A lot of information is available in written form, whether on the internet, in periodicals, or in books. So what could be better than trying to learn some techniques of selecting and remembering this information more quickly? Various speed reading techniques have been developed which help to accomplish this goal. They give you the ability to have a more or less in depth contact with the subject matter. If you master speed reading technique, then the practice of mnemonics is an optimal way for you to retain the information.

Task:

Learn to speed read. Learn several methods and find out which ones work best with which type of information, so that you can productively take in as much information as possible in the shortest amount of time. Also make sure that along with this knowledge, you also obtain skills that you can apply in your life.

Variations:

* Find other ways of processing information more quickly. Use the mind mapping method to structure the information.

2.15 Trial Lessons!

Pretty much everywhere today, it is possible to try something out for free, just to get a feel for it. Opportunities such as trial periods at the fitness studio, free evening seminars, or continuing education events abound. Online you can find free e-books on many subjects, online courses, and online tutorials. Many of these only cover material by way of introduction, but this is more than enough for this exercise.

In large cities there are tutorial groups in every possible subject, many of which are free. These are great chances to get to know new people and things. I once organized a tutorial group in my home town, and every evening it went differently, with new people in attendance, with all kinds of interesting situations. At the end of many of the free trial lessons you will be asked if you would like to continue. Think about it for at least a week before you decide.

Task:

Take at least an hour a week to do a trial lesson. Do whatever you can find, whether it has interested you before or not. Remember that you can find these trial lessons in various fields of interest, such as sports, music, continuing education, languages, etc.

Variations:

- Offer free trial lessons for your favorite hobby.

- Look for free trial lessons online, in the form of online courses or e-books, on subjects that you have perhaps never been interested in.

2.16 Focusing!

Psychologists discovered long ago that our emotions are not dependent upon the situations we are in, but upon how we value those situations, and how we handle them. You decide in every situation how you are going to react. We often respond to situations just because of habits which we have developed over the years.

Everyone can change these habits. Many believe that they have to get annoyed when someone cuts in front of them, unaware of the fact that they could deal with it differently.

With this exercise you should find out for yourself the best way for you to respond to various situations. For this purpose, in the next few days, you can try out two extremes, seeing how each effects you. Do the different reactions make a difference for the rest of your life?

Task:

Think negatively for one week. Complain about everything around you and be unhappy with everything. Find reasons why others are always guilty and why you can't do anything to change the situation.

The next week, think only positively. Be friendly to everyone, and bring good cheer wherever you go. If something doesn't go as you hoped it would, think about how you can change something, and do it.

Observe yourself very closely in both weeks and find out what effect each way of thinking has on you.

2.17 Housekeeping!

According to the book Clear your clutter with Feng Shui, having orderly surroundings is important. Karen Kingston is of the opinion that order is essential for the proper flow of energy, allowing us to reach our full potential. She includes basements, closets, etc. According to her, even small areas of clutter, like desk drawers, can have a negative effect on us.

Even though Feng Shui presents only one explanation, it is still important for you to try out for yourself what does and doesn't work.

I always used to hear that an organized desk is better, so I decided to give it a try in an attempt to create my optimal working environment. Doing so gave me a lot of clarity regarding my way of working, and how my surroundings affect it. You should do the same.

Task:

Make sure that your desk is always unorganized for a whole week, and work at it.

Make sure that your desk is always neat, that means completely empty, except for your computer, and the document you are working on. Notice in which environment you feel more comfortable or are more productive.

Variation:

- Do this exercise with your apartment.

www.comfortzonebook.com

2.18 Childhood Fun!

Do you remember how as a child you met so many new situations without any problem? And how much fun you had in doing so? From a certain age, we discover that our behavior is not considered appropriate. We learn that there is supposedly right and wrong behavior. So others decide for us what is right and wrong, and through praise and censure they impose their opinions upon us.

It is time for you to reconnect with your inner child, and to start integrating it into your life.

Task:

Go out in the pouring rain, run through the puddles just so that they splash, laugh, and enjoy seeing the bewildered faces of those passing by. Try to get as wet as you can, and then take a hot shower or bath.

Act like a child. Beg for sweets in the supermarket. Enjoy life. Climb all over everything, jump rope, play, use every playground, and take pleasure in the little things in life.

Variations:

* Observe a child and try to perceive the world in the same way as they do.

2.19 Be Mystique!

In the X-Men comics and films Mystique, a shapeshifter, appears again and again. She can change her outer form to be anything she wants, and she can be whoever she wants to be. Wouldn't that be something for you?

Mark Twain once said, "Clothes make the man." I have come to the realization that when I dress differently, those around me respond to me differently. When I wear a suit, people look at me differently than when I wear my old comfortable clothes. In some clubs there is even a dress code, which you have to obey if you want to be let in.

Task:

Dress up, styling yourself like someone who is younger or older than you- as a punk, a techno fan, a Goth, a banker, a contractor, etc. Notice for each one the different ways that people respond to you. When you wear different clothes, does something change in the way you think and present yourself?

Variations:

- Go to work in a different style than you have before.

- Go to a costume rental store and rent the costume of a person you have always wanted to be.

www.comfortzonebook.com

2.20 Powerless!

Almost no one is aware of how much their daily life is dependent upon electricity. Just think about it- all that you can't do without electricity. It begins as soon as you get up. You don't have an alarm clock, you can't turn on the light, and most people have to take a cold shower. You can only make a yourself coffee or tea if you have a gas oven. Your refrigerator won't work anymore, so you have to go shopping every day, just to have fresh food.

Your mobility is also greatly limited, since you don't have any more cars, buses, or trains to get around in, so you have to depend upon your own legs, whether walking, biking or skating. At evening, at the latest, your day is over.

Task:

Live a few days without electricity. Don't use any electrical appliances.

2.21 Our Daily Movie!

Actors are used to slipping into different roles, and appearing before the public. Not many people know that today almost everyone plays a role, most of the time unconsciously. A good example of this is at work. This exercise involves leaving your normal behavior behind and acting, just like an actor. Remember that with acting, the role is not the same as the person.

What roles are expected of you over the course of the day? In the tarot game, there is the card of the fool, which stands for lightheartedness. The fool can play any role, and only because of this is he a trump card.

Task:

Today, play a different role from the ones that are expected of you at the moment.

Variations:

- List the roles that you think are expected of you. Switch the roles around with one another.

2.22 The Black List!

Here is the ultimate exercise, for the end of the section, Breaking the Routine.

At the end of the day a lot of people can't say any more what they did the whole day and where all the hours have gone. If they thought about it, they would slowly come to the realization that they have used the majority of the time in a more or less meaningful way. However the real time wasters are many times the mindless activities that we do again and again.

Task:

Take something to write with and make a list of all of the activities of your day. Activities like brushing your teeth, dusting, watching TV, reading, smoking or eating. Categorize each item under the headings "Good for me," and "Less good for me."

Now mark all of the things that you don't think are meaningful, which limit you or keep you from doing something important. Decide which activities you want to give up in the future, and which ones you are going to limit. Use the time you have freed to do something worthwhile. I am sure you will find enough suggestions in this book.

Variation:

• Start new habits which you think will do you good.

3 Self Confidence

Here you will find many exercises which will help you to gain more self confidence.

3.1   Who let the Dogs out?

What does taking the dogs out have to do with leaving your comfort zone? There are people who are afraid of dogs, but that is not the reason for this exercise.

Just yesterday I saw again how a young woman was taken for a walk by her dog. Dogs only respond to clear signals and dominance. They want to know who is in charge, or otherwise they will take the leading role. With this exercise you will learn not only to overcome your fear of dogs, if you have it, but you will also learn how to send clear nonverbal signals, and also become a more self confident and vibrant person.

Task:

Go to an animal shelter in your neighborhood and take a dog for a walk. Be sure that the dog is at least medium size. Ask for a grown dog, which is attentive and follows clear signals.

Variation:

*   Take care of a dog for a week.

www.comfortzonebook.com

3.2   Be a King!

Nowadays many of us aren't used to receiving courteous, friendly treatment. I realized this at the supermarket around the corner. There was a lady at the cash register who wished me a good evening, but with her voice she gave the impression that she didn't really mean it, and that it didn't really matter to her at all how my evening was. So to say good bye, I decided to compliment her, as described in exercise 1.7. I thanked her, wishing her a wonderful evening from the bottom of my heart. It surprised her, and she blushed slightly. Right then I knew that I had to go someplace where I would be treated in a courteous, hearty, and friendly way. I used to think that to be treated this way I had to be somebody important, at best someone with a lot of money, until I found out that being rich or famous is not a prerequisite for being treated really well.

My idea was the following: why not just have a cup of hot chocolate in a five-star hotel? OK, perhaps it costs a couple Euros more, but I figured that I had earned it. So I made my way towards the Four Seasons hotel in Hamburg. Besides having excellent service and a really wonderful atmosphere, I got a hot chocolate which really lived up to its name. Instead of just a regular hot cocoa, a thick and chocolaty liquid went down my throat, an experience unlike any I had had before. Since then I have regularly treated myself to a luxury hot chocolate. It was interesting for me also to see how creative and productive this helped me to be, in these luxurious surroundings. And it gave me a real boost on the business projects I was working on. Is there really such a thing as money energy?

Task:

Drink your next coffee, tea, or your next hot chocolate in a really nice Café, restaurant or hotel, and enjoy the way that you are treated.

Variations:

- Go to the luxury car or sports car dealer and pretend to be a potential customer. Take a test drive.

- Have a real estate agent show you the house or apartment of your dreams.

- Go into a really good clothing shop and have them give you advice, and then try on an whole new outfit. Pay attention to how you are treated, and what a difference this makes in the way you present yourself. In the process, you might even decide to change how you dress.

www.comfortzonebook.com

3.3 Hollywood ist calling!

We live today in a world where one can, and sometimes even has to, appear publicly without great effort. Nevertheless, many people are too shy to use this new opportunity. Today, Hollywood is everywher...

Task:

Make a film of yourself and put it on www.youtube.com or another internet platform.

Variations:

*   Go and sing in a karaoke bar.

*   Make a film where you embarrass yourself and put it online.

3.4 Style your World!

This exercise is very similar to exercise 1.5, but this time it is not about changing your style, but about attracting positive comments about yourself. What do other people appreciate about you? What do you get praise and compliments for? How do you handle them when you receive them?

For this exercise, use your experience from exercise 1.5.

Task:

Every day, go into a different clothing store, and have the salesperson tell you what your positive qualities are and how you can bring them out. Change your style by using the information you have gained. Give the most weight to the feedback from professional fashion advisors, and those who are important to you.

Variation:

•   Ask friends and acquaintances to help you with this.

3.5   The Bourne Identity!

One trick that has been used for centuries, by all sorts of people, is changing your identity. With another identity, you try out some amazing things, and you have the advantage that if anything bad happens, then it is connected with this other identity and not with you.

This exercise isn't about assuming another identity to take advantage of someone. It's really about having experiences that are different from your ordinary life. This can help you find where you want to go in the future, and what you enjoy doing the most. It is also interesting to observe how the behavior of your conversation partner changes just because of the information they receive regarding your identity. And interestingly, when you change your identity, it seems that something changes in your own personality...

Task:

Make yourself business cards with different identities, such as art dealer, creative strategy specialist, philosopher, photographer, jack-of-all-trades, trainer, etc. Remember that some titles are protected and you can't take them. Live with this identity, as though it were your true identity, and see what happens and how the people you speak to react.

Variation:

*   Think of some names that you always have liked, and introduce yourself with one of them for a while.

3.6   The Expert Builder!

Studies in psychology have proven that people put their trust more readily in someone who holds the title of "expert." To take advantage of this fact, it isn't so important at first to be a real expert, but to be considered an expert. The path to being an expert has two parts. The first is being convinced that you are an expert, and the second is competency. This exercise is about reaching the first step of expert status as quickly as possible.

In this exercise you will need abilities that you have gained through the previous exercises, such as making contacts. Becoming an expert is not hard. But in performing this exercise, I strongly suggest that you don't try to pretend to be someone who you aren't. But who decides then who is an expert? It isn't about the number of titles you hold, or abilities you have, but it's about the cultural environment- in contexts such as the media. The media often defines who is an expert and who isn't. Other criteria which are consulted are contacts, references from clients, salesmanship, vibrancy, media savvy, and many more. Use these and become an expert in the area of your choice. Through this exercise you will hopefully be able to convince yourself that you are an expert, without forgetting that in order to be a true expert you also have to be competent.

Task:

Chose a special field in which you want to be an expert. Give yourself 1-3 months time to learn the core knowledge in this field from magazines, books, etc. Prepare to give a two hour seminar about this area. This should give you the necessary confidence.

Variations:

•   You can find assistance with becoming an expert in the list of websites at the end of this book.

•   Acquire the knowledge and the abilities that characterize an expert.

3.7   Hero!

Most people are well acquainted with what they are not able to do so well, what they have failed to accomplished, and so on. Many lie awake at night in bed thinking about what they failed at again during the day, forgetting about everything that they've accomplished. So often, we focus on our mistakes. We learned this during our time in school, where the focus was always on the mistakes we made. What we did wrong was always being pointed out, but almost never what we did right.

In addition, modesty is now considered a virtue in Germany, and whoever is confident in himself and his abilities is often written off as arrogant. But when you think about it, every one of us is a hero.

Task:

Write a biography about yourself, where you explain why you are a hero. List all of the things that you appreciate about yourself, what others appreciate about you, everything you have accomplished, and so on. In case nothing comes to mind, ask those around you what they appreciate about you, what they consider to be your strengths, etc.

Variations:

*   Make a success diary! Every evening, write all that you have done very well, what you are proud of, and why you had a great day. For this, use a nice, expensive notebook, such as Paperblanks.

*   Write yourself a love letter.

3.8 Live your Dream!

This exercise is based upon exercises 3.4 and 3.5. The difference is that this time you don't just assume another identity, but you act as if you were the person you have always wanted to be. Imagine that you have already achieved all you want to achieve. How do you feel? What do you think? What are you going to do? Where and with whom do you want to live? During one coaching session I asked a coachee to imagine that he had already reached the goal of his life, and to tell me how he felt, and what he thought. He found out for himself that his envisioned goal wasn't really his life's goal after all, and that reaching it wouldn't make him any happier than he was at the moment.

The exercise requires some fantasy and a kind of schizophrenia, but it can be a lot of fun. More than anything, it helps you to discover whether reaching your life goal really would make you happy. You have of course the chance to try out several different sets of goals.

Task:

What is your life's goal? Live it for at least a week. Imagine, that your surrounding is the one where you would live in then. Go for a walk there and sit down in one of the locales. Have a realtor show you your dream home, as described in exercise 3.2. Who would you be? What would your business card say? How would it feel to be this person? What would you do in this role? How would you talk, and how would you dress? Do anything that helps you to feel and to act like this person.

Variations:

- Try out other goals, including some that you are not right now trying to reach.

- Organize a success party, where everyone acts as if they have already achieved what they want to achieve, and can prove it.

3.9 Do an Internship!

Many people have the same job for their entire lives. But because they never take the chance to try out many other jobs, they don't know if this job is the right job for them. The tendency is to change jobs regularly, but usually just to get one that is better paid. But how about trying out a different job altogether?

This exercise gives you the chance to try out some potential lines of work without commitment. In high school in Germany, students have to complete one or two internships. But the question is, is two enough? Unfortunately, for most of them, it is not. There are also many people, who after years in their professions come to the realization that their profession is not fulfilling for them. So it is a good idea to at least see what other jobs are like.

I just wanted to say a word regarding salary. You are of course aware of the fact that different professions are paid differently, and that most people make their decisions based upon with which job they will make the most money. But is this a way to decide how you are to spend your time, whether you enjoy doing it nor not? Or in other words, can money buy you happiness?

Task:

Look for internships in professions which you have always found interesting. Complete an internship. If you are working, try to do it during your vacation time.

Variations:

*   Do an internship in a profession that you never wanted to do.

*   Offer an internship in your company, so that others can get to know your profession.

3.10 Be different!

Our life is often influenced by the expectations of those around us, for example at the office, from the partner, from the family, or from friends. These expectations are invisible and are very often unrecognizable.

Expectations only exist in relationships between people. The company doesn't expect you to act in such and such a way, but rather the people working for the company. And perhaps they expect this because they believe that it is also expected of them. Now some people try to benefit through expectations imposed by society. Unfortunately, this doesn't always work to your benefit. Psychologists have discovered certain patterns, where clever techniques can be used to manipulate others. Someone just presses certain buttons in order to produce the desired responses. The advertising world is full of people who take advantage of this phenomenon.

In this exercise, you will free yourself from these expectations. That doesn't mean that you will now become socially unacceptable, but that from now on, it is you who will decide consciously what you do and why you do it.

Task:

Make a list of things which you think are expected of you, such as coming to the office in a suit. Even in partnerships, certain expectations are established after a certain amount of time. Break through the rigidness of these expectations, and take the time to speak with your partner about them.

Variations:

- Go shopping in your pajamas or your bathrobe.

- For one day, say no to all requests that are asked of you.

- Shave your head.

3.11 Move your Body!

Our human personality is shown, among other things, through our body language, or the way we move. There are scientists who believe that we can change our personalities by changing the way we move. For example, if a shy person usually takes small and quiet steps, and then begins to go around taking big, firm steps, then the corresponding character trait changes as well. In this exercise you have the chance to find this out for yourself. What kinds of movements are comfortable for you? Which movements aren't? Which movements seem to have an impact on your personality?

Some might object that through these changes we will no longer be ourselves. But we have learned all of our movements when we were children, through unconsciously observing our parents and siblings. Thinking about it like this, it's time to change the way you move.

Task:

Think about how you move. Film yourself when you are walking, standing, sitting, etc. Observe people who you feel have magnetic personalities. How do they move? Try to move more like they do, long enough for you to start feeling comfortable doing so. How do you feel now? How do people respond to you? What changes do you recognize?

Variationen:

- What do you notice about the way your favorite actors move in different roles?

- Think about someone whose personality or appearance is not attractive to you for some reason. How do they move?

3.12 Babel!

Almost everyone has learned a foreign language in school, which may never get used except on vacation. Language researchers have investigated
the effects that speaking another language has on how we respond to
the world around us. They took a survey with certain questions, where those participating had to answer first in their native language, and
then in a foreign language. They found out that in answering the same
question, but now in a foreign language, other parts of the brain become
active, ones different from those that are responsible for speech. And the
answers showed that the participant's opinions were different depending on the language that they were speaking. The emotions that usually
were attached to certain topics were not the same as those as when
they answered in their native language. The researchers concluded that
in our native language, certain words are associated with certain feelings
(connotation). For example, for most Germans, the word "arbeiten" (to
work) has a negative connotation. But using the English verb, "work,"
seldom produces any emotional reaction at all.

We will further explore this phenomenon in this exercise.

Task:

Take advantage of every possible opportunity to have a conversation
in a foreign language. If needed, make some opportunities for yourself
by joining conversation groups. Watch films in the original language and
communicate in foreign language forums on the internet.

Variation:

*   If needed, communicate with your hands and feet. Nonverbal com-
    munication is a way of conversation.

3.13 Charity!

Every year, shortly before Christmas, it seems like we are constantly being asked to give money. Everywhere on the street, people are coll- ecting donations for one thing or another. Sometimes they are abused by those passing by. In spite of this, most of them stay in a good mood, and continue on towards their lofty goal. The purpose of this exercise is to have you make yourself available to a good cause, and then have you take a stand for something. And in the process, don't let the reactions of the people you attempt to solicit cause you to lose your confidence, but continue to pursue your goal.

Task:

Look for a meaningful cause for which it is meaningful to collect dona- tions. Unfortunately, there are too many of them to mention. Then, stand in a busy spot, and ask those passing by for donations. Donate everything that you receive.

Variations:

•   Go to businesses and ask for donations.

•   Beg for the money, and then donate everything to charity.

3.14 Reciting Poems!

Working with one's comfort zone is meaningful in many areas of life, and now it is even making its way into the field of psychotherapy. For example, so-called social phobias are treated with special exercises, such as the following. We very often make our actions dependent upon others, and their opinions of us. With social phobias, this pattern is very distinct. These fears have been unconsciously developed in our childhood.

The goal of this exercise is to make us more independent of what we imagine to be the opinions of others. In any case, we can't know for sure what others think about us. We interpret it subjectively. It is up to us to evaluate ourselves in a constructive way.

Task:

Choose several poems which you find meaningful. Then go to a busy street or shopping area, and recite them aloud, with the proper delivery style.

Variations:

•   Sing the poems, or sing songs which you think are tasteful.

•   Tell some exciting stories in public.

3.15 Improve yourself!

The improvisational theater was developed by Keith Johnstone in the middle of the 20th century. It is more and more often used in the area of personal development. Through exposure to constantly changing roles and situations, you train your spontaneity, your flexibility, and your ability to communicate with body language.

The theater will produce visible improvements in your personal development.

Task:

Look for an improvisational theater and participate in one.

Do some online research to find some improvisational theaters in your area. In many cities, beginner courses are offered. Sign up for one of them.

Variations:

*   Start your own improvisation group, learning all you can along the way.

3.16 Share!

It is often useful to compare the way you see yourself with the way that others perceive you, in order to get outside feedback, and to discuss your experiences with others. The internet is the ideal place for this. You can present and discuss many subjects online, doing so anonymously if you wish.

Forums, blogs, and video hosts like YouTube thrive because of the growing online community. They give everyone the chance to post questions on every subject, to share thoughts with others, to discuss, and to publish videos and photos. There are even people who have become stars through the internet.

Task:

Record yourself doing the exercises in this book, and post the videos online. Post a link to the site hosting your videos on the comfort zone forum, or send it to the authors. In the comfort zone forum, you can also post a comment regarding your experiences with the exercises, along with any new ideas for more exercises.

www.comfortzonebook.com

3.17 Johnny Mnemonic!

Before the invention of the printing press, knowledge was a very valuable commodity, only possessed by a handful of people. Books had to be painstakingly transcribed, and most knowledge was passed down through oral tradition. Nowadays, however, there is the tendency everywhere not to memorize anything at all, but just to look the information up right away on the internet, or some other source of information. Despite this, the technique of mnemonics is having a Renaissance, and in many places, this ancient technique is presented in a new way and sold as some kind of a magic bullet.

Earlier on, people memorized things they were learning by using mnemonics. Today, mnemonics is widely represented in countries where illiteracy is widespread. It has been determined that illiterate people have a much better memory than those who depend upon the written form of communication. And a good memory is still quite useful today in many situations, don't you think? If you are interested in the history of mnemonics, then I suggest the book The Art of Memory, by Frances A. Yates, a prominent historian. In her book, she describes the development of mnemonics, including fascinating descriptions of the systems of geniuses, who could visualize entire libraries, being able to bring their entire contents back to mind.

Task:

Learn some mnemonic techniques, use them, and train your memory.

Variations:

*   Develop your own memorization techniques based on mnemonic techniques. Think, for example, about "memorable" places like libraries, and visualize them in your mind. This serves as a starting place for your mnemonic technique.

3.18 Strange Words!

Nowadays, in everyday conversation we use a maximum of 800 words, and if we learn another language, we only need between 100-300 words to make ourselves understood. To read magazines or take college classes, you need a more comprehensive vocabulary of 5,000 words. While a tabloid uses a vocabulary of around 400 words, other newspapers use around 5,000. Just by changing the newspaper you read, you can easily expand your vocabulary. The vocabulary that Goethe handed down was made up of an astounding 90,000 words.

Your flexibility is expressed through how you speak. The larger your vocabulary, the better you can express your personality. The more bizarre and remarkable the word, the more effort needed to employ it in a conversation. And after doing this long enough, no one will be able to beat you at Scrabble.

Task:

Learn a new word every day, and use it ten times throughout the course of the day. Do this for at least one whole month. Start with words that correspond to the way you speak, and then start to use more complicated words.

Variations:

*   Learn the new words in a foreign language at the same time.

3.19 Hold a Lecture!

So many people are afraid of public speaking. No matter why this may be, now is time for a change. Presenting yourself and your knowledge before an audience requires and creates a great deal of confidence. But to do this, you really have to believe that you have something to say.

You can also learn how to captivate the audience, draw them into a story, and make them laugh. When you succeed at doing this before a large crowd, then it becomes even easier to accomplish in a small group or in a one-on-one conversation.

Task:

Familiarize yourself with a theme of your own choice, and organize a lecture which lasts for at least two hours, with an audience of at least 20. You can decide for yourself whether or not you want to charge money for those who attend.

Variations:

•   Prepare to speak about something which you do not even like to speak about, and give a lecture on it, as described above.

•   Record your lecture with a video camera, and then analyze it. What was good? What can you do better? Remind yourself of what was covered in exercise 3.11.

3.20 Mentoring!

We often underestimate just how much we have learned in our lives. Many think that their abilities are not special, and that everyone can do the same things that they can. OK, it is very likely that there is always someone who knows more than you in one area or another, but taken altogether, your knowledge and your experiences are unique to you alone. And just as there is almost always someone who is more knowledgeable and experienced than you are, there is also always someone who is less knowledgeable and less experienced, who could greatly profit by learning from you.

Task:

Ask yourself the question, "In which areas of my life could others profit from my knowledge and experiences?" Then look for one or several people to mentor, and accompany them along the way, passing along your experience and knowledge.

Variations:

•   Look for "virtual" mentors, who are willing to assist you online by e-mail, for example.

•   Register at www.bbbsd.org as a mentor, and help children.

www.comfortzonebook.com

3.21 Tell the Truth!

Do you know the film Liar Liar? In this film, Jim Carrey plays a lawyer, who because of his son's birthday wish, can only tell the truth. Because of this, he ends up in all kinds of interesting situations. Most of us probably don't even realize how often in the day we tell a lie, to avoid an uncomfortable situation. But now let's bring the truth to light...

Task:

For one day, tell the truth. In really explosive situations, such as conversations with your boss, you can naturally consider saying nothing at all. Lies are not allowed, not even white lies.

Variations:

* Do this for a week.

3.22 V.I.P. Alarm!

More than 90% of the people consider themselves to be average, and cannot imagine that they are destined for something greater. The other 10% are different from the rest, not because they have rare abilities, but because they simply have another way of thinking. This 10% set very high goals for themselves, which result in a real change in their thought structures.

Have you thought it possible up until now to speak with a celebrity, without having someone else make the connection for you? No? Then you will soon see that impossible goals can actually be very easy, if you have the proper mindset.

Task:

Contact the celebrity of your choice. Before you do, think about a question you can ask. The question should reflect genuine interest, as though you were well acquainted with them, not just a fan. Take an interest in their work, and not in their private life.

www.comfortzonebook.com

3.23 Create Art!

Who actually defines what art is? The journalists who write about it in the newspaper? Joseph Beuys with all of his works of art have emphatically proven that art always depends upon the perspective from which it is approached. They have also proven that anything can be art.

With this in mind, anyone can make art. So what has been keeping you from making art of your own?

Task:

Make your own work of art with the things in your surroundings at the moment. Take a few hours of time and transform them into art. Think about a name for the piece that you just made. Go to a shopping area with your newly created works of art, and display them, explaining to the people passing by what they represent and why they have artistic merit.

Variations:

•   Find galleries in which to display your art.

4 Relationships

Here you will find a few exercises that should strengthen your relation-ship.

4.1 Look me in the Eyes!

The eyes are the windows to the soul. Through the eyes a deep connection can be made with someone, conveying thoughts and emotions. Right after they have fallen in love, couples are still in the habit of looking each other in the eyes. Over time, this becomes less and less frequent. Some studies have even shown that many people in a relationship can't even remember the eye color of their partner.

Back in exercise 1.1, you had the unique experiences of looking strangers in the eyes. Now it is time, once again, to intensively look your partner in the eyes. Not while you are just telling them how your day was, but with your complete attention upon them, and being conscious of the bond between the two of you.

Task:

For 4 weeks time, take at least ten minutes a day to look your partner in the eyes. Make sure that you aren't distracted. Sit across from each other in a comfortable atmosphere, and look at each other in the eyes for ten minutes. Be quiet and monitor your thoughts and feelings. Afterwards, speak about what you experienced.

Variations:

- While doing the exercise, breathe with the same rhythm.

- Look for a really nice place to do this exercise.

- Hold each other's hands during the exercise.

www.comfortzonebook.com

4.2 Eat in Darkness!

After focusing on the sense of sight in the previous exercise, this time we will go without it completely. In today's world, a lot of attention is paid to visual impressions. Because of this, our other senses are dispro- portionately challenged and stimulated. When we close our eyes for just a few minutes, we already begin to perceive the world differently. This can at first make us feel uneasy, but gradually our other senses become sharper. Allow yourselves as a couple to come into a world where you have a more acute sense of smell- a world which you can feel, taste, and enjoy together.

Task:

Choose a meal to cook together. Set the table and make the room completely dark. Make sure that you have complete silence. If the room cannot be made completely dark, then blindfold yourselves with sleeping masks, so that you can't see anything at all. Then eat the meal you have made with silverware.

Variations:

- Feed each other.

- Eat without silverware.

- Go to a dark restaurant and spoil yourselves in darkness.

- Prepare your meal in the dark as well.

4.3   Praise your Partner!

In exercise 1.7, you gave compliments to strangers, friends, and acquaintances, and you learned what reactions they provoked. But why
travel so far away, when happiness is so close to home? Now that we are
able to see the good qualities in other people, and how to accentuate
the positive by using words of praise, it's time to use these abilities to
make our partners happy.

This exercise also helps you to reacquaint yourself with your partner's
nice qualities, perhaps things you have never noticed before. Sometimes
it is the little things which seem make us the most happy.

Task:

Give yourself 4 weeks, where you give one another at least five sincere
compliments a day, as described in exercise 1.7. During this time, also
go without accusing, blaming, or making any comments that could make
them feel guilty.

Go without anything that could give your partner a bad feeling, and do
everything you can think of to make them feel good.

4.4 Poetry Slam!

Hundreds of years ago, it was still common for lovers to express their feelings with songs, poems, romantic ballads, and other ways in writing. Many of these works are still able of rekindling feelings of romance in our hearts, giving them a place amongst the greatest cultural treasures of mankind.

In the previous exercise, you have found out what desirable qualities your partner offers. So what could be better than recording some of these attributes for posterity, allowing your partner to enjoy them again and again?

Task:

Write your partner a poem. Write it on really nice paper, with the best pen that you have. Maybe you even have a quill or fountain pen. Write only kind things and avoid anything that is negative.

Variations:

*   Write a love letter.

*   Write the poem or love letter in calligraphy.

*   Present your results aloud.

4.5   One Hour Love Week!

Since the earliest times, certain practices or rituals were used to help to ensure the quality and health relationships. After having been practically forgotten for a time, they are now coming back into the vogue. To really open up to someone also means that each person gives the other their undivided attention. For this it is important to take the necessary time. This doesn't mean just to spend time together, but to use the time with and for one another. This is of course difficult to do while sitting in front of the television. In exercise 2.11, you already have had the experience of going without entertainment and the media, so that part shouldn't be a problem. The purpose of this exercise is not for you to act in a stiff way towards one another. If you normally never watch TV, then it can of course be nice to watch a film together and then to talk about it. This exercise is just about turning your attention towards one another, and spending time with each other, instead of only in the same room. Enjoy having one another close by, and show each other how much you en-joy each other's company. Laugh together and have precious moments together, which you will remember for a long time. Then, experience moments like these together again and again in your daily life.

Task:

Take at least an hour every week to concentrate only on your relation-ship. Schedule this at a special time, and make sure that you set aside this time just for yourselves. Then take turns deciding what to do during this time.

Variations:

*   Massage your partner for one hour. Next time switch.

*   Stretch out time which you spend together by a half an hour every week. You don't have to spend all of this time together all at the same time, because maybe your schedule is too tight. However, when you do set aside the time, the time together should last for at least an hour.

4.6 Dialogue!

The idea of dialogue originally comes from couples counseling. It is supposed to facilitate the communication of the ongoing pressures and strains of life, with the hope that they can be resolved in dialogue. It is a self-help concept, which is conducted without outside help. What is wonderful about it is its ability to further deepen a good, stable relationship. In relationships, it is possible that a lot of consideration is given to the other person, sometimes too much. Nowadays it is considered improper to talk only about yourself. In a relationship, however, it is important that the other person knows what is happening inside of the other, and how they are doing emotionally. In the dialogue, one's own perspective should be communicated to the other. So in this conversation, avoid speaking from the point of view of your partner. The dialogue is to take place regularly, always lasting a given amount of time. I've read of people who have been doing these dialogues for years now, whose relationships are very happy.

Task:

Set aside 60 minutes for the conversation, making sure that no one disturbs you. The first partner has 15 minutes, where they speak exclusively about themselves, without any interruption from the other partner. For 15 minutes, they are supposed to answer the question, "What concerns me the most at the moment?" It makes no difference whether or not the conversation is related to things inside or outside of the relationship. Once the 15 minutes are up, the roles are switched, and the next 15 minutes belong to the other partner. Afterwards, you can each take one more turn speaking, so that each of you speaks twice. You should speak about your experiences on the next day, at the earliest.

Variation:

* Take 90 minutes time, and each take one more turn speaking.

4.7 Falling Down!

In so many relationships, the partners would like to be able to fall down, and then be picked up again. This is usually understood in a figurative sense, but in this exercise we are going to take it literally. The same principles apply, in any case.

Here you will learn to trust your partner, to let yourself go, and to realize that you will be picked up over and over again.

Task:

One of you stands behind the other, with the one standing behind taking a stable position. At first, don't stand too far apart. When they are ready, the person standing in the back signals the person in front. Then the person standing in front lets themselves fall back, allowing themselves to be caught by the one standing behind them. Repeat this procedure several times, each time increasing the distance between you. The time elapsed, while one of you is actually freely falling, increases each time. Go only as far as to allow the person in the back to comfortably catch their partner. Then switch positions.

Variation:

•   When one of you is too heavy for the other, then get the help of someone you trust.

4.8 Blind Trust!

Trust is one of the most important foundations for a happy relationship. Trust can be divided into two categories: trusting one other, and trusting oneself.

Exercises for developing one's own self-confidence have been covered already in chapter 3, so here the focus will be on trusting one other.

Task:

Decide who is leading and who is being led. The one who is leading has the responsibility for the other. The one who is being led is to be blind-folded. Then, you as the leading party are to guide your partner through life for a whole day, being there for them constantly, taking care of them, preparing their food, leading them everywhere, and giving them all of your attention and love. Then some other day, switch roles.

Variations:

•   Decide beforehand what you want to do during the course of the day (under the same conditions as described above, of course).

4.9   A Day in Bed!

When newly in love, couples can easily spend a whole weekend in bed together. But once the daily routine starts to take over the relationship, the time spent together becomes shorter and shorter. Then, when children are added to the picture, most people find it very difficult to set aside any time for each other whatsoever.

With this exercise, you have the opportunity to remember the time when you first fell in love, to experience and to enjoy it again.

Task:

Spend a whole day together in bed. Make sure that you are not interrupted for the entire time. Prepare the food beforehand, so that you just have to get up quickly to get it, and then eat it together in bed. You could also order your meals, to make this easier. Speak about the finer things in life, and leave the daily routine behind you. Give each other royal treatment, with kind words, caresses, and massages.

Variations:

*   Spend a whole weekend in bed.

*   Go without any kind of entertainment or media which could distract you from one another.

*   Spend the time in the dark, or blindfolded.

www.comfortzonebook.com

4.10 Give a day!

Over and over, we enter into compromises in our relationships, which in the end please no one. How about giving your partner an entire day, where you do anything they tell you to do? But the most important thing is, that no matter whether it is really your favorite thing to do or not, that you have fun doing it.

Let your partner sense that you do it gladly and that the thing that is most important for you is to make him happy. To do this, you might have to put your own needs and desires aside. You shouldn't expect anything in return.

Task:

Give your partner one day. He decides what you do, and you just have fun. Take care of everything necessary for the day to be a success, so that you talk about it for a long time.

Variations:

- Überlege Dir, womit Du Deinen Partner glücklich machen könntest und organisiere einen Tag für ihn.

- Do something together that you have never done together, or have never done at all.

- Organize such days regularly.

5 Physical Borderline Experiences

You can leave you comfort zone with your body too.

5.1   Extreme Sports!

When it comes to leaving our comfort zones, a lot of people think about the exercises that we are about to encounter- physical extreme sports. These are experiences only recently made available to us, due to advances in technology. With these exercises, some of our primal fears are brought back. These fears are present for each of us in varying degrees. So I suggest that you try out all of the variations one by one. Perhaps you will even come up with some of your own. Unfortunately, performing these exercises can be very technically demanding, so they are at least somewhat expensive. If money is a problem, then think of a way to use one of the other comfort zone exercises to help you to some extra cash. Maybe you can find a way to do the exercises without spending a lot of money. For ideas, just take a look at www.immerleben.de.

Task:

Take a look at the variations and do them one after another. Be conscious of how you feel before, during, and after each one. If you feel the inclination to put off one of the tasks, then you should purpose to do it as soon as you possibly can. Notice what effects these exercise have on your life.

Variationen:

- Go rappelling.
- Go skydiving.
- Go hang gliding or paragliding.
- Go climbing.
- Go diving.
- Play with snakes, spiders, etc.
- Jump from a 10 meter high tower.
- Do similar things to these.

www.comfortzonebook.com

5.2 Just do it!

Unfortunately, just doing regular sporting activities is leaving their comfort zone for some people. This is even more astounding, when you consider that for years now, it seems like everyone is becoming more and more interested in fitness and health. I don't want to try to convince you of any of the hype, but you at least have to you try it out, and see if it is good for you or not.

In case you already are doing sports fairly regularly, you can use the opportunity to try out some new varieties of sports. I find it especially important to try out sports which are usually played only by the opposite sex. Also, try out different kinds of team sports.

Task:

For the next 4 weeks, do sports at least 2 times a week.

After you have done this, look for a team sport that normally doesn't appeal to you, or is normally associated with the opposite sex. If you are a man, you can try aerobics or a lower body workout. If you are a woman, try soccer. Try out a variety of sports. You can take trial lessons for this purpose, most of which are free, just like you did in exercise 2.15.

Variations:

•   Go to sporting event that normally doesn't interest you, such as a football game. The more spectators, the better.

5.3   No Food!

Fasting is natural, but in today's indulgent society, it has been largely
forgotten. Anyone can fast. Sometimes it just needs a little warm up. The
more often that one fasts, the more quickly and more easily the body
can switch over to fasting. Fasting is one of the fundamental human experiences.

When you fast, you can have very unique experiences. When I fast, I
need a lot less sleep. Usually 3 hours a day is enough. I also have the
feeling that I am bursting with energy, and it is easier to be creative. If
food didn't smell and taste so good, I would enjoy fasting almost all of
the time.

In any case, regardless of your health, you should only do this under me-
dical supervision. Ask your doctor beforehand, whether your body is in
the proper condition for fasting. If you have health problems, fast anyhow,
but look for a fasting partner, something more and more common in
Germany. This person knows all about the potential problems that can
arise during fasting, and the best way to handle them.

A time of fasting is a time where you are strongly confronted with yourself. You can intensify this through doing some of the below variations.

Task:

Get information about fasting. Find out what you are supposed to watch
for and do before, during, and at the end of the fast. Fast for at least a
week, but if you can manage 14 days, then that is even better. If during
the first time, you can only fast for a week, then you can fast for 14 days
later on. Pay attention to how it makes you feel. Over the course of the
day, how does the way your body feels change? Use the time and energy
that you gain with a purpose. How do you feel afterwards? What changes
do you sense?

Variations:

- Mediate while you fast. (Exercise 5.4)

- Withdraw from the world during your fast (Exercise 2.11, 7.2)

- Work with your plans for your life.

- Work creatively.

- Do Yoga or Pilates.

5.4 Meditation!

Besides fasting, one of the best ways to get in touch with oneself is mediation. Mediation has had a very long tradition, and can be found again and again in every culture. It existed before the discovery of the wheel, the fire, or the invention of script. The power of meditation was discovered and was used as early as the Stone Age. Over time, meditation became a basic part of the culture of many people groups. In some religions, meditation has remained the focus, whereas in others, it is prayer.

When we meditate, we develop our minds and gain insight into our inner selves. Mediation brings our minds to ease, in times when our days are filled with stress. Many famous people today have rediscovered the ability to draw energy from meditation.

Through mediation you will become more sensitive to your physical condition, also learning to better accept the state of your body. By meditating, you activate the undeveloped potential of your brain and discover what is hiding inside of you. You also find out about your own individuality. Meditating can also help you to deal with difficult situations in life, to let go of traumatic experiences, and to lead you to inner peace. Even if in the beginning, it is hard for you to quiet your mind and get used to it, meditation is well worth it.

To meditate, you don't need any outside assistance, much less money. You just need to close yourself off from the world and be quiet.

There are many different ways to meditate, and different ones work for each person. Do some research about them, and look for the one that seems to work the best for you. Try out several different options, in case you are not so sure. You might come up against some resistance. Withstand it. More specific directions about this subject, and about different meditation techniques, can be found on the site referred to in the text.

Variations:

- Yoga

- Autogenic Training

- Guided visualization

- Looking into a flame

5.5 Boxing!

When children get into a scuffle, grownups often look at as something negative. But apparently it is important for our development, since it is something we all have had the desire or tendency to do at some point. Of course it isn't good when stronger children use it to take advantage of weaker ones. But on the other hand, fighting can help give us self-confidence and control of our bodies, as it can also help train our reflexes. It also helps us to develop our strength, helping us to get rid of excess energy and unwanted stress.

In doing this exercise, make sure that you don't start fighting against each other, but rather with each other. The goal is not to hurt the other person, but to bring them to their physical limits.

Task:

Look for the opportunity to climb into the boxing ring with a friend, acquaintance, or even a stranger. Put on protective clothing. Keep boxing, without stopping for breaks, until one of you gives up.

Variation:

* Organize a fight or scrimmage in part of your apartment which you prepare accordingly. Protect yourself as much as possible, using blankets and pillows.

5.6   Floatation Tank!

A floatation tank is an enclosed room, filled with salt water, where one is completely isolated from all outside noise. The salt water is kept at skin temperature, which gives you the impression that there is no gravity.

The floatation tank is currently the only way to experience some time free from all outside stimulation. There are no influences upon your thoughts from outside, because you are surrounded by silence and darkness. You don't feel any environment because the water and air inside the tank are set to body temperature and the high salt content of the water allows you to float. You become oblivious to all that is going on outside of the tank. The tank is sound and light-proof, so you are confronted with yourself alone.

You can utilize this opportunity as a way to help you to observe your inner world, which is visible to you through your thoughts.

Task:

Spend an hour in a floatation tank. There should be one in every large city. Did you manage to become absolutely still, or were you constantly thinking? What were you thinking about?

Variations:

*   Meditate (see exercise 5.3).

*   Focus on a certain problem or task and try to invent a variety of solutions.

5.7   Sweet Life!

In most of the foods we eat every day, there are addictive substances. Most of us are either unaware of this fact, or we ignore it intentionally. Sugar and coffee are the best examples for this. I would guess that more than 80% of Germans are addicted to sugar, whereas well over 50% are addicted to caffeine.

I am not trying to keep you from drinking coffee or eating a piece of chocolate. For me, I just see the importance of the freedom of being able to decide what you eat, independent of food addictions. But for this to happen, you have to break the addiction to begin with.

I used to be strongly addicted to sugar. Every day I just had to have a chocolate bar, an ice cream, or something of the sort. Many times, at night I would eat a couple of 200 gram (7 ounce) chocolate bars or a liter of ice cream as well. Then it occurred to me, that I wasn't doing this just because I liked the taste, because I could enjoy the smaller amounts just as easily. Besides this, I noticed that these amounts weren't helping me at all. I was becoming lazier and lazier, and was gaining more and more weight. I was spending the evenings in front of the television with bags of candy in my hand. But I did not feel good at all.

Even though I realized this, it was very difficult for me to become free from sugar addiction. I was always falling back into the habit. At some point, I managed to survive for two months without sugar, and suddenly I had no more cravings for sweets. Nowadays, I eat a piece of chocolate or an ice cream cone every once in a while. But I enjoy this to its fullest. I no longer feel compelled to eat whole chocolate bars in one sitting. I consciously make the decision of whether or not I want to eat something sweet..

www.comfortzonebook.com

Task:

For four weeks, go without any kind of drugs. No coffee, no cigarettes, no tea, no alcohol, no sugar, no white flour, no television. In case you can't manage to abstain from all of these at once, just stop the intake of one, then the other. It is important that you manage to get by without these drugs for at least 4 weeks. If you give up sugar, then also abstain from other sweeteners. Only natural fruit sugar (fructose) is allowed.

Variation:

* For four weeks, eat a vegetarian or vegan diet.

5.8 Work Physically!

We live in a so-called information society. Most jobs nowadays use only our mouths and our fingers. This isn't physically demanding for many people at all. Even on the way to work, we barely move. We go with the car, or with the public transportation.

Again and again, I have seen the benefit and satisfaction that hard physical work can bring. When we work physically hard, our body releases happiness hormones. After the day, you have the opportunity to look at your day's work and to see what you have accomplished with your own hands. After you are done, your sleep becomes much deeper and more relaxing. During physical work, many of the muscle groups are automatically trained, helping to reduce stress.

Task:

Work for one week in a job such as farmhand, carpenter, or a construction worker.

5.9 Sweat Lodge!

The sweat lodge (also called a purification ceremony) was originally used in Native American rituals, as a way to maintain physical health, and for inner cleansing. When going into the sweat lodge, fears, stresses, and inhibitions are brought up to the conscious level. Once you recognize them, you can observe them, isolate them, and work on them intensively in the time to come.

Being in a sweat lodge is much more intense than being in a sauna. You are inside much longer. It is usually very uncomfortable and tight, depending on the number of people participating. And as if that weren't enough, it is extremely hot.

After my first time in a sweat lodge, I was in a state of euphoria for quite some time. While inside, I wanted to give up many times. I forced myself to endure it. I was glad I did. We all realized that the experience had just had really brought us beyond the borders of our comfort zones, testing our physical capacities in an extreme way. Even for those who use the sauna regularly, it was a big challenge. It was a remarkable experience.

Task:

Look for a place near you that hosts a sweat lodge ceremony.

5.10 Go the Way of St. James!

Lately, the Way of St. James has become famous in Germany because of the best-selling book by Hape Kerkeling, which has inspired many people to try taking a trip on the Way of St. James for themselves.

Choosing to go the way of Saint James can be a borderline experience for the body. This depends largely upon the distance you travel each day. A friend of mine traveled on the way of St. James for two weeks, each day walking 30 to 40 kilometers. Part of her wanted go back and to give up, but she didn't want to expose herself to ridicule. After she had endured a couple of hard days, a certain euphoria set in, which made carrying the 45 pound backpacks seem effortless. When she returned, she was very proud of her achievement. She converted a lot of fat into muscle, and she knew that she wanted to do it again.

Task:

Take a hike along the way of Saint James. Depending on how much time you have, look for the best possible starting point, one which will take you to your limits, forcing you to strive to achieve your goal within a given time.

Variations:

- Go out for hikes or bike excursions, which last for at least two weeks, daily testing your limits.

- Train for a marathon, and then participate in it.

- Bike to the top of one of the highest mountains of the Tour de France.

6 Traveling

Only through traveling can you truly leave your comfort zone. But there are ways to take traveling to even greater heights :-)

6.1   Be interested in Culture!

In all of my trips, I have realized that many people visit museums and other cultural establishments in a foreign city, without ever having taken the opportunity to visit the ones that are in their own cities. This is a pity, because if only they had invested the time in discovering art in their home cities, then they would really be able to appreciate it more on their trips.

Many people visit museums just to be able to say something like, "I have been to this museum. Here are the photos to prove it." The art itself is actually secondary. A while ago, I was in Rome with a friend. He had studied art there for a half a year, and he helped me to see art in a completely different way. He asked me, for example, why the Laokoon-Group is so famous. What makes it special? He also made me compare famous statues with some less famous ones. He helped to train my eye to see the paintings in a different way, so that I could learn how to recognize the uniqueness of each painting, and to understand its place within the history of art.

One doesn't need to travel to do this. In Germany we have many museums with many famous works of art. While you are in your home city or home country, you have the chance to visit the same museum many times. This allows you to concentrate on a few exhibits each time, and to really take a closer look. You can spend time comparing the works of one artist with another, to help you to understand his development as an artist. You can also compare the masterpieces of one time period with another, to see the reason why certain artists became famous. These artists all had one thing in common: bringing something new into the world.

Task:

Go to museums, theater, operas, classical concerts, exhibitions, musicals, lectures, libraries and so on. Before you go, research as much as you can about the subject of the event. When there, take all of the information that they give you, and try to immerse yourself in the subject. Why are those works of art so special? If you do not understand something, then find somebody who can explain it to you.

Variations:

*   Compare different cultures with one another.

6.2 Don´t be afraid of the Unfamiliar!

Many trips are not so much about experiencing new things and getting a taste of something different, as they are about recording these experiences in the form of pictures, movies, etc. It seems like it is all about being in a certain place and then having something to prove it, rather than experiencing the place itself.

As mentioned before, I was in Rome, where along with many others, I was waiting in the long line in front of the Vatican museum. When I finally had the chance to see the great masterpieces of Michelangelo, Rafael, and the other masters, with my own eyes, they made a tremendous impression on me. For many of the people in the museum, the whole point of coming to the museum was to take pictures of the various works of art. They came, took a picture and then left. They never really even looked at what they were photographing.

They took pictures because their guidebook told them that they had to see certain things. But in choosing to heed this advice, they missed out on the beauty and the intensity of the works of art themselves. Instead, they produced all kinds of low quality pictures, which could be considered art. But anyone could have bought the pictures in books, which are always for sale, and gotten much better pictures. I for one did not take many pictures, and we will soon see what a difference this can make.

By not using your camera, you give yourself the possibility of experiencing the world firsthand, instead of filtering everything through a camera lens. You put yourself in the situation where you must take a snapshot in your mind. Then, when you get home, you have to bring back to mind all that you saw, and what really made an impression on you, instead of just showing people pictures. By going without your travel guide, you will find tourist attractions of your own, that perhaps no one else finds interesting. You can discover the area yourself and find out what you like, and what you feel is worthwhile.

www.comfortzonebook.com

Task:

Choose a time to travel without using any technology. The best thing you can do is travel without a travel guide. Discover the area on your own. Ask the local people what their favorite spots are, where they like to relax, or take in other cultures. Basically, ask where they spend their free time. Once you have found something you enjoy, put together information about it, as you did as described in the exercise 6.1.

Variations:

• Just let yourself go anywhere you feel like going, and see where you end up.

6.3   The Weekend is calling!

With the technical possibilities that we have in today's world, it is very easy to explore the world for a very small price. 200 years ago, it took weeks to travel through Europe. Even after the invention of the railroad, it still took days. But today, for just a few Euros, you can fly between the metropolises of Europe, take a tour through the city, and then fly back. The time it takes to fly from Prague to Berlin is less than the time it takes to drive from one side of Berlin to the other. So why should you deprive yourself of these opportunities?

Most employees and workers in Germany have around 30 days of vacation. But in addition to this, they have over 100 days of weekend. Instead of thinking about what you should do in just a few weeks of vacation, you can just learn how to take advantage of some of your many weekends. Naturally, these trips cannot be taken too far from home. On the other side, in our own area (flights between two and three hours included), there are plenty of rewarding travel destinations. Discovering these alone could take a lifetime.

I am not talking about just traveling for the sake of traveling. Let the trip become an experience, just like in all of the other exercises.

Task:

Organize a weekend trip once a month.

Variation:

*   Every month, discover the things in your area, either by foot or by bike. Each time, expand the limits of the area that you have explored.

6.4   Poor vs. Rich!

On vacation, everyone wants to go all out. After all, you have been saving up for half a year, and looking forward to it for so long. But what does it mean to go all out? A five-star hotel, with everything included? Or is it just about just enjoying something? How much does this enjoyment depend upon the setting? You can find out the answer to this in this exercise. Traveling doesn't have to be carefully planned and scheduled. Spontaneous trips, which can last for only a few days, can sometimes be a lot more exciting. In my last vacation, I spent the first five days in a four-star hotel in a wonderful area. I spent the next ten days in bunk beds in a room with ten other people, with only one bathroom. You can guess where I had the most fun, meeting the most interesting people- people with whom I am still in contact...

Task:

Make your lodgings on your next vacation flexible. Stay overnight in a hostel, and with the money you save, stay one night in the best hotel in the city. Eat as cheaply as you can, and then you should be able to afford a meal in the best restaurant. Save money during the trip, and then splurge on a business or first class ticket. Get in touch with people everywhere and find out what kind of people they are, and how happy they are in life. Watch how you feel in different situations. Try to determine how much your happiness depends upon your environment, and then see if you can learn to be content wherever you are.

Variations:

• Go on vacation one time in a monastery

• Travel once by train instead of flying or driving.

• Go by bus or hitch-hike.

6.5   Learning the Language!

Time and time again I notice that people in the countries that I visit respond positively, even if I say only few words in their language. Suddenly they behave very differently toward me, and act as if I weren't just an ordinary tourist.

Since I realized this, I have developed the habit, before I travel, of learning at list a couple of phrases in the national language. Over the time, I have managed to learn all kinds of foreign phrases. Often it is enough to have a basic vocabulary of between 100 and 300 words. Then, if you only adjust to the melody of the language, it will be very easy for you to make yourself understood in different countries.

Task:

Learn the language of the country that you want to visit. The longer you will stay there, the more words you should learn. Learn 20 words and phrases for every day that you want to spend there. Use your new language skills on your trip, and try to just speak the local language to communicate to the people there.

Variation:

- Every time that you are confronted with another culture, learn ten words in that language. For example, if you go out to eat Italian, learn ten words of Italian.

www.comfortzonebook.com

6.6   Play Travel Guide!

Again and again, I notice how people go on vacation and go through the city with a tour guide, just to see the tourist attractions. The funny thing is, though, that many times they never find the time to see the sights in their own cities.

A little while ago I was visiting Berlin again, where I have come to know my way around fairly well. At the end of my trip I really wanted to see the district of Friedrichshain. So I asked some people who had lived there for a while, "What should I definitely see in Friedrichshain?"

It really surprised me that none of them could give me any substantial information. Is this the same for you in your city? Then now is the time to change that.

Task:

First, discover the tourist attractions in your own city or area. You learned how to do this in the previous exercises.

Then, offer your services as a free travel guide, advertising on websites such as www.couchsurfing.org

Variation:

*   Acquaint yourself with the most important tourist attractions in a city other than your own. Then you can try to get a job as a tourist guide there.

6.7   Get to know the Locals!

Even if there is a good tour guide available, the best way to get to know a country or a city is to ask the people that live there. They know the best places to visit, where the people are the nicest, and when the best time is to visit certain places.

Over time, I have come to know a lot of people in many cities, with whom I can go out, whenever I am in their neighborhood. In many cases I can stay overnight at their homes.

Use the local language as often as you can, when you start a conversation. This breaks the ice most of the time. The ability to make contacts, which we practiced in the first exercises, is very helpful in this.

Task:

Get to know some local people who can take you around when you are staying someplace out of town. It doesn't matter if it is a vacation, a business trip, or only a visit.

Variations:

• Try to get invited to parties in a foreign city.

• Stay overnight with strangers. In the list of links at the end of the book, you can find websites that help you to find people who will let you stay overnight at their homes. This gives you the ability to stay somewhere for very little money, and also allows you to make contacts at the same time.

6.8 Travel alone in a Foreign Country!

Traveling alone in a foreign country is one of the most exciting activities of all. Everyone should do this at least once in their lives, because the experiences that you can have doing this, makes it worth everything.

Task:

Travel to a country you have always wanted to see. Pack everything you need, and travel alone. To help you to do this, there are very good English speaking tour guides available at Lonely Planet.

Variation:

*   Travel from hostel to hostel and connect with other travelers. Set a budget for the day, including your overnight expenses, for say 20 Euros.

7 Mastery Exercises

Here you will find the exercises that probably only very few people will ever do. But you have come to the last chapter in this book. If you have done all of the exercises so far, then a bit of time has already past, and hopefully this book has been your companion through it all.

From my experiences, and from the experiences of the people I have gotten to know, I can imagine how exciting your life is now. I am sure that it only slightly resembles the life you lived before. The transformation techniques connected with these exercises have made an impression on your life like a blueprint, and boredom or lack of social contact is now a thing of the past. You are also approaching unfamiliar situations with a different perspective.

But despite of all this, there are still even more opportunities for you to bring your personal development forward. The development of your personality never stops, even in a very advanced age.

Now come the exercises which probably only very few will ever do. Maybe you are one of those few. :-)

7.1 Vipassana Meditation!

This exercise is a combination of many of the ones we have already co-vered, as are the majority of the other mastery exercises.

Vipassana mediation is one of the oldest forms of meditation. For vari-ous reasons, we put it in this last group of extreme exercises. The parti-cipation requirements bring most people to different places, far outside of their comfort zones.

The hardest thing for me is not to communicate for ten days. Not with other participants, and not with friends and acquaintances outside of the course. That means not only is talking not allowed, but neither is any form of nonverbal communication. Also, every form of distraction is also forbidden. No sports, no reading or writing, especially not the use of media devices such as mp3 players, cell phones, and so on. Vegetarian meals are prescribed, and every person mediates about 11 hours every day alone or in a group room. You can find more information on the list of links.

Task:

*   Study the participation requirements very carefully, and then regis-ter for a ten-day Vipassana mediation course.

7.2   A Weekend in the Forest!

In his book, Walden, Henry D. Thoreau speaks about how he made it in the wild for 2 years. He withdrew from the industrialization which was beginning at the time, in order to achieve an alternative, more balanced lifestyle.

We are living in something close to paradise, where food is practically flying into our mouths. Only very few people nowadays would be able to take care of themselves in the wild. But with this exercise you can change that, by proving that you can actually survive on your own.

Task:

Learn how to live in the forest, what you can eat there, and how you can build a shelter. Go for one weekend, only with the things you can carry on your body, and survive there alone.

Variations:

•   Live for a week alone in the forest.

•   Take your children with you, if they are old enough, and teach them how to survive in the forest or in the wild.

7.3 Everybody's Darling!

With this assignment you can escape the ever-increasing anonymity of the city, and get to know new people every day. Besides this, this exercise prepares you for even more to come.

In this exercise, you will learn not only how to meet new people, but also how to change your charisma and your appearance so much, that you will appear nice to most people, and they will let you stay overnight with them, without knowing you. To do this, you will have to first train your attentiveness. Second, you must either consciously or unconsciously recognize what makes your conversation partner tick. You have to find out what to say or how to behave, in order for them to think that you are a nice person. So find something you two have in common, and try to bring this out. With this exercise, certain things will occur to you, with which you can win the sympathy of your fellow humans.

Task:

Speak with strangers on the street, and ask them if you can stay over their house overnight. Then sleep over at these people's houses. Use the opportunity to get to know these people better. Why did they let you stay overnight with them? Are they happy? Why or why not? What is the one thing that is most important to them?

7.4 Limited Money!

Every time I tell people about my trips, I hear the question, "How can you afford to manage that?" My answer every time is that money is not needed in order to travel. It is helpful and makes some things simpler. But what is really needed, in order to be able to travel, is flexibility and courage. In the last two exercises I have already given you some tasks that have helped you to develop these abilities. This exercise also prepares you to do what you want to do and not to be dependent upon money.

Task:

Survive for a week in any city with only 10 Euros. If you decide to do this in your home city, then pretend that you are in a foreign city. Do this by pretending that you have no apartment or friends for the time being.

7.5   You travel, I pay!

And here comes the mastery exercise you have all been waiting for!

It sounds really tempting: I will pay for your trip. You read it correctly.
I will pay the costs for a trip that you take. Naturally there are certain
conditions that apply. Of course, you have to prove that you are a master
of leaving your comfort zone, and that you have been able to succeed in
accomplishing most of the exercises in this book. Almost all of the experiences that you have had from the exercises in this book can be applied
during this trip into a new world. I don't want to talk too long, but get
you going right away. Now let's go!

Task:

Take 20 Dollars and find your way to Shanghai. Travel only from the 20
Dollars you brought along, and from the money that you earn on the
trip. If you manage to arrive in Shanghai and to return on this 20 Dollars,
I will pay for your trip. And you will get a certificate from me giving you
the title, "Master of Comfort Zone Expansion."

7.6 Guerilla Marketing!

You have now arrived at the last exercise of the book. How does it feel to have expanded your comfort zone so much, along with your horizons?

The fact that you have come so far shows me that you really must like the exercises. I would venture to say that they have had a strong influence on your life. Even if you might not have tried all of the exercises with all of their variations, you are probably still already totally amazed. So with this exercise, you have the opportunity to allow other people to take part in these experiences.

Task:

Use the exercises in this book to help others. Do Guerilla Marketing, using exotic promotion tactics. If this book has helped you in your development, then you can naturally also help to spread the word about the book, helping it find its way to more and more people. Develop strategies to help spread the word. How could these people profit the most from this book?

The Authors

Sascha Ballach:

After his education as a computer specialist, and in the studies which followed, Sascha Ballach worked successfully as a software developer for several well known companies. His life's dream, to work with people, to help them in their own personal development, and to effect real changes, has been something he has been working on in the past few years.

Sascha is a NLP trainer, hosts regular NLP exercise nights, and runs his own blog about the subject personal development. In his seminars, in his coaching, and working with himself, he has developed the concept of the comfort zone exercises, and along with Andreas Brede, is constantly working to improve them.

Andreas Brede:

Andreas Brede is passionately active as an NLP-trainer, having been working with NLP and personal development since 2001. Along with various seminars, for many years he has been leading an independent NLP-peer group in Stuttgart. His special way of making NLP and personal development real to other people is due not so much to teaching certain techniques, but to activating people's resources and expanding their comfort zones, thereby increasing their quality of life. He has become well known for his intuitive and empathetic style in the transformation work.

In his free time, he devotes himself, along with other pursuits, to music. He is a member of the band "Solveig Songs", has his own solo projects and his own recording studio.

Get out of your Comfort Zone even further

If you want to know more about the topic of leaving your comfort zone, personal developement or random acts of kindness, then visit the site www.comfortzonebook.com. Here you will also get a list of over 60 inspiring movies for free.

There will also be an App which we are developing at the moment. This App is for Iphone and Android with many more exercises. In the last months and years I collected a lot of different exercises for various areas of your life and I will put them all into this App.

Visit our website and try it out:

www.comfortzonebook.com

Notes

Notes

Made in the USA
San Bernardino, CA
18 January 2016